FANTASTIC
FUTURE

**DR MIKE GOLDSMITH**

*Illustrated by*
*Daniel Postgate*

Scholastic Children's Books,
Commonwealth House, 1–19 New Oxford Street,
London WC1A 1NU, UK

A division of Scholastic Ltd
London ~ New York ~ Toronto ~ Sydney ~ Auckland
Mexico City ~ New Delhi ~ Hong Kong

Published in the UK by Scholastic Ltd, 2004



ISBN 0 439 97336 8


Printed and bound by AIT Nørhaven A/S, Denmark

2 4 6 8 10 9 7 5 3

# CONTENTS

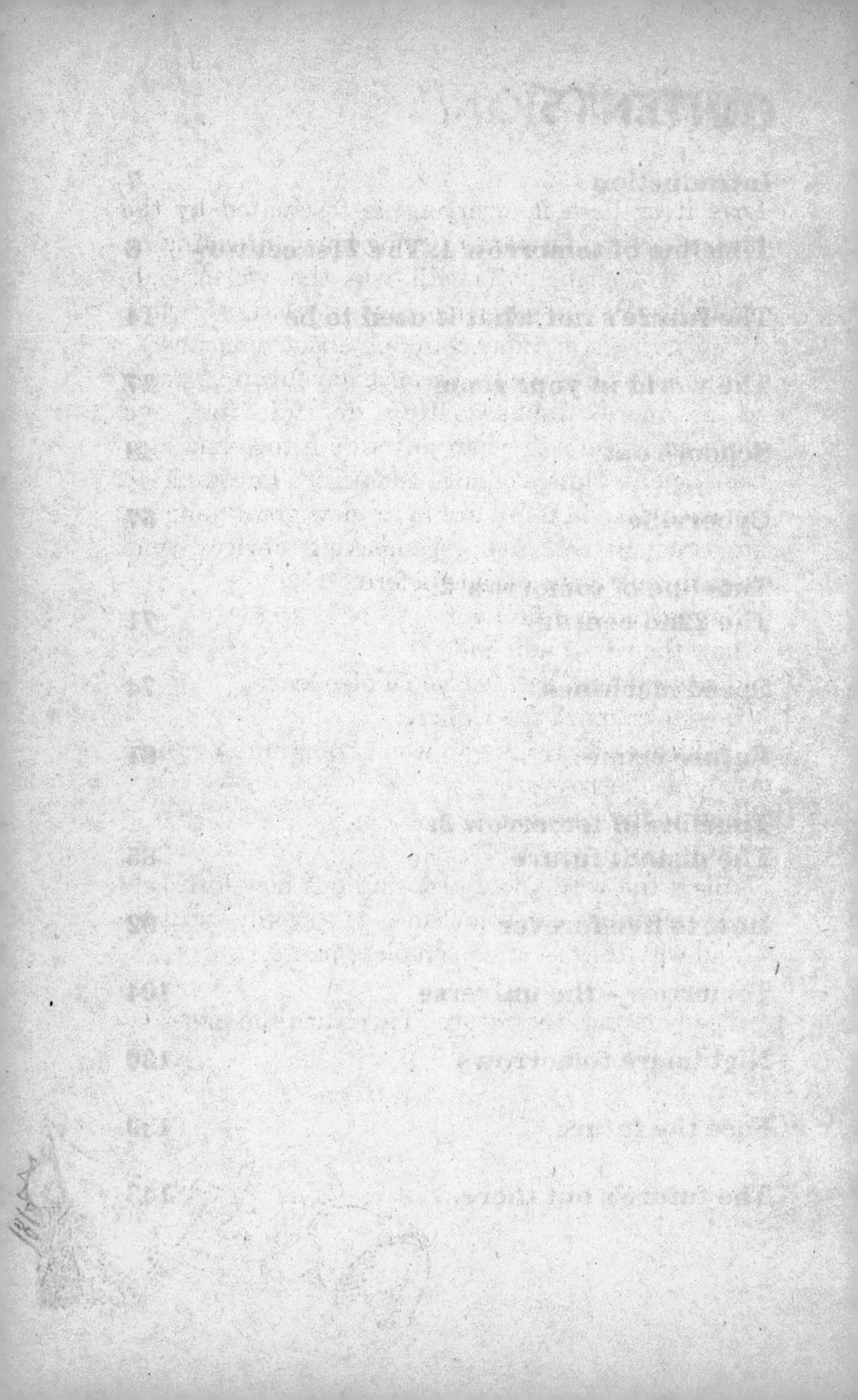

# INTRODUCTION

Love it or hate it, everyone is fascinated by the future: looking forward to going home, dreading an exam, wondering who will win the World Cup, planning the perfect crime, buying a lottery ticket, we spend a lot of today thinking about tomorrow.

And it's just as well – because our future is going to be more flabbergasting, fearful, fun and altogether fantastic than anyone's future has ever been before. Things change so fast, it's hard to keep up: each decade there are more new great gadgets, gorgeous gizmos and gobsmacking devices than were invented the decade before.

So read on and find out:

• how the world will end;

but never mind, because you'll also learn:

• how to colonize the Galaxy;

and in case you think you won't be around by then, you'll also discover:

• how to live for ever.

Along the way, you'll also find out how forecasts and predictions can sometimes be spookily accurate – and why they're often complete pants.

Ready to face the future? Then turn the page...

# TIMELINE OF TOMORROW 1: THE 21ST CENTURY

By tomorrow, I don't mean the day after today, I mean the decades and centuries and millennia ahead. There is a lot of scary stuff lying in wait, as well as some amazing advances – but before you get too excited and/or hide under the bed, it's worth remembering that some of these things are a long time off yet.

The near future is fairly easy to predict – better mobiles, faster computers, more robots – but just imagine what the world will be like in a few thousand years. The future is full of mysteries that only time can answer, but the ideas in this book aren't just wild thoughts – they're predictions, which are mostly made by studying how things have changed in the past and working out the effects of those changes as they continue into the future. This idea isn't new – in fact, over 2,000 years ago, a Chinese thinker named Confucius said:

Working out *what* will happen is much easier than working out *when*. Most of the things in this book are very likely to happen – but a lot of the dates are probably not quite right. For instance, people are almost bound to land on Mars one day – we already have the technology to do it. But it will cost a lot of money and it's very difficult to say exactly when people will decide the trip is worth the fare.

Let's start off by looking just a short way into the future, to the things you can expect to happen this century...

**2010** You are watching a new film starring actors who died before you were born – thanks to better, faster, more intelligent computers. But you're not in a cinema – it's on your mobile, which also contains your favourite books, notes, photos and videos.

**2011** You leaf through your favourite magazine – which has been personalized so it only contains what you want to read and look at. It's even got your name on the cover.

**2012** You have a smart card that you can use as a door key, passport, driving licence, bus pass and credit card. It also contains your medical records and lots more about you. It makes life easier for you – and for the government to keep tabs on where you are and what you do.

**2013** Footballers all wear tiny cameras and microphones during the game so viewers can watch from their favourite player's point of view – for a price.

**2015** Robots are clever and reliable enough to be given jobs as basic fire-fighters, security guards, cleaners and gardeners – so you see them all over the place. In fact, you're so used to them you hardly notice them any more.

**2018** Tiny machines called MEMS (MicroElectroMechanical Systems), not much bigger than grains of rice, are all over the place. They have built-in microphones, thermometers and other instruments and can communicate with each other and with their control centre. They use signals from satellites to work out where they are, and they're used for things like monitoring forest fires, keeping an eye on the weather, measuring how noisy roads are, finding out how dirty the sea is, and warning when planes, railway tracks and buildings are getting ready to fall apart.

**2020** A lot of the world's energy is produced cleanly and safely: the wind, the waves, the rivers, the light of the Sun and the power of volcanoes are harnessed and converted to electricity. There is a small base on the Moon.

**2025** In rich countries, there are more robots than people. They work in factories, on farms, underwater and in the home – and they're also used to fight battles, including battles with other robots.

**2030** The Moon base has grown and now includes a small hotel for rich tourists. The base looks like a collection of plastic and metal huts under a sealed transparent dome. Some parts are underground, in natural lunar caverns. Near the Moon's south pole, in a deep dark crater where the Sun never shines, there is an amazing telescope, which enables the viewer to see planets around other stars.

**2035** Humans have landed on Mars and spent several months there, in a base built for them in advance by robots.

**2040** Almost all diseases have been cured by genetic engineering. There are cloned dinosaurs in zoos.

**2045** Space junk – worn-out spaceships, dead satellites, empty fuel tanks, old bits of space station – is becoming a major problem, mainly because of the risk of collisions with spacecraft, satellites and space stations. Enormously powerful lasers based on the Moon are used to slow down the bigger pieces of junk, so that they fall to Earth, burning up on the way down in the form of spectacular meteor showers.

**2050** Some robots are more intelligent than people. We're still surrounded by computers, but few have keyboards – because there are much easier and more natural ways to access them. We speak to them, wave at them, even think to them. In fact, a lot of machines are thought-controlled, thanks to sensitive detectors that recognize the brain waves we make when we want something. The detectors send radio signals to whatever machines we want to control.

**2060** There is now a permanent Mars base.

**2070** There are almost no forests left – just about all of them have been wiped out for their wood and to make space for vast farming areas. No people work on the farms, only robots, directed by computer systems that are cleverer than we are. There are riots and demonstrations from time to time, by people frightened at the prospect of super-intelligent machinery. (In dark factories and under the streets, maybe that machinery is laughing to itself.)

**2075** The Moon and Mars bases have grown into large colonies by now, with some inhabitants who have been born there. Sooner or later, it's likely that the colonies will try to become independent of Earth – which might lead to the first interplanetary war.

**2080** Lots of people are over 120 years old.

**2085** People can make any animal or plant they can think of, thanks to genetic engineering: the must-have Christmas present this year could be a pet you design for yourself. Accidents and sabotage are likely to lead to the birth of monstrous creatures – which might escape from time to time.

**2090** Genetically manufactured viruses are used to make plastics and to break them down again when they're thrown away.

# THE FUTURE'S NOT WHAT IT USED TO BE

We're living in yesterday's tomorrow today – and it's not quite what your grandparents expected in the 1950s. We *do* have: mobile phones, skyscrapers and plenty of robots – and these were all predicted back then. But we *don't* have: atomic planes, flying cars or food pills

– though at the time these seemed just as likely. The thing is, predicting is tricky – though some bits of the future can be calculated, and some can be guessed, a lot can't even be imagined.

## Time tracks

Some things can be foretold with incredible accuracy – for instance, in 2020 in December at 13 minutes past four in the afternoon there will be a total eclipse of the Sun, and a bright comet will appear in the sky in November 2061.

Why is this? Why are some things, like the time of an eclipse, so utterly predictable and others, like whether it will be too cloudy to see it, so utterly *not*?

Here's a little list to explain...

**1. Completely predictable things**

**Examples:** eclipses, high tides, some comets, sunrises. These are predictable because scientists understand exactly *why* they happen. Take sunrises. Even thousands of years ago, people had quite a good idea when the Sun would rise over the next few months. Any farmer gathering his crops in autumn would know that the Sun would be rising a bit later each morning until midwinter, when it would start to rise earlier. Some people had the skill to measure the times of sunrise and, once they'd made enough measurements, they could use them to work out when the Sun would rise in the future.

To make this sort of prediction, it didn't matter that people didn't know what caused sunrise (some thought the Sun was dragged across the sky by a god, others that a new sun was made each morning, others that the Sun orbited the Earth).

But the answers were only roughly correct. However, by the 16th century, scientists knew that the rising of the Sun is caused by the spinning of the Earth, and that the exact time of sunrise depends both on the Earth's spin and the way it moves round the Sun. Because they also knew exactly how the Earth moves, scientists could make exact predictions of the times of sunrise years – even centuries – ahead. Once people take the step from knowing *what* happens to exactly *why* it happens, really accurate predictions become possible. Unfortunately, a lot of stuff we're interested in predicting depends on things which we don't understand exactly – like why people change and react and behave the way they do.

**2. Very predictable things**

**Examples:** the number of meteorites that'll fall next year, the number of people who will win £10 in the lottery next month.

Given a nice large amount of information, predictions about the near future can be made quite accurately by a science called statistics. For instance, by analysing thousands of exam results, the number of people who are likely to get a "B" in maths next year can be worked out very accurately. But the answers are only of limited use because they can't tell you what result any *particular* person will get. Also, this only works for predictions about the fairly near future: over decades or centuries, things like exam results, amounts of rainfall, numbers of people with colds, life expectancies and lottery-ticket sales change significantly.

**3. Fairly predictable things**

**Examples:** the power of computers, the population of the Earth, the amount of ice round the poles.

Even where things *do* change over time, rough predictions can still be made, by looking at the way they have changed over long periods in the past. For decades, deserts have been spreading, the Earth's population has been getting larger, computers have been getting more powerful and forests have been being cut down, so it's fairly simple to predict how such things (called trends) will change in the future too.

Some of these predictions are surprisingly good: in 1965, it was predicted that computer power would double every 18 months, just as it had up to then. And so it has, ever since! The big problem with predicting by using trends is that, sooner or later, most trends stop. For example, for many years there have been five people born every second, while only two have died every second – so the population of the Earth has been growing at a rate of three people every second. But this just *can't* go on forever – at that rate, the Earth's population will double in the next 35 years, and will be ten times its current size in a century. If the trend continued, there would be 1,000 times as many people on Earth in the year 2300 as there are now! But this seems impossible – there is a limit to the number of people the Earth can support. So, one day, the trend will end.

There are various sorts of trends, and some are quite tricky to analyse. A *linear* trend is one where something increases steadily (like the Earth's population), or decreases steadily (like the number of people with a black-and-white telly). Other trends are *cyclical* – meaning that something rises and falls and rises and falls over and over again. Cyclical trends include things like ice-cream sales, which go up in summer and down in winter, or the world's temperature, which gets right chilly every hundred million years or so.

**4. Slightly predictable things**

**Examples:** humans living on Mars this century, people watching TV over their mobiles within five years, chatty robots in your lifetime.

In many ways, people don't change much over time – they want to explore, communicate, feel safe, make friends – so developments that help them do those things are likely to happen. This is true even if the things people want don't really make much sense – for instance, there's really no need to send humans to Mars. Robots can do a lot more than astronauts can, for a fraction of the cost. And yet, nevertheless, people just really *want* to go there, so there's a fair chance that, one year soon, they will.

**5. Things which aren't predictable at all**

**Examples:** next year's number-one single, who will win the next World Cup, whether it will rain on 22 May 2024, whether a coin will fall as heads or tails.

These things are so unknowably mysterious you might as well not bother – because there are no rules for any of them.

## Time explorers

People who try to study the future in a scientific way are called forecasters or futurologists (unlike people who study it in unscientific ways – they're called prophets or fortune-tellers). Forecasters concentrate on things in the near future that they can predict fairly well – like the weather tomorrow, or the number of burglaries that will happen next year. Forecasters are employed by supermarkets so they know how many sunglasses or scarves or umbrellas or copies of the next *Harry Potter* to order.

Futurologists, on the whole, look further into the future than forecasters – decades or centuries ahead rather than days or months. They are employed by governments and by big companies who need to make long-term decisions, answering questions like: is it worth investing ten years of research in a solar-powered bus? Well, maybe – IF solar cells become more efficient, IF people still want to travel by bus in ten years' time, IF fuel prices go on rising. Futurologists try to answer these iffy questions. Not surprisingly, they don't always get the right answers.

***Flashback***

*If it weren't for futurologists, we might only now be recovering from a massive worldwide computer breakdown that happened on 1 January 2000, and caused planes to fall from the sky, economies to collapse and people to starve. In the late 20th century it was realized that, because computers used to store dates in the form 01.01.99, rather than 01.01.1999, they could go completely haywire when the new millennium began, because their clocks would try to go back: to 01.01.00. Because this problem was predicted, an international effort to reprogram the world's computers succeeded – just in time.*

There are some things about the Universe which make a futurologist's job tough. Or, in some cases, impossible. Let's look at some of them:

## Tricky predicting 1: A guide to chaos theory

Imagine you're sitting on top of a mountain. All you have with you is a very large bag of stones. You roll one stone after another down the mountain. For a long time, nothing happens – each stone rolls down a bit and stops. But, eventually, maybe after the 98th stone or the 723rd or the 9,332nd...

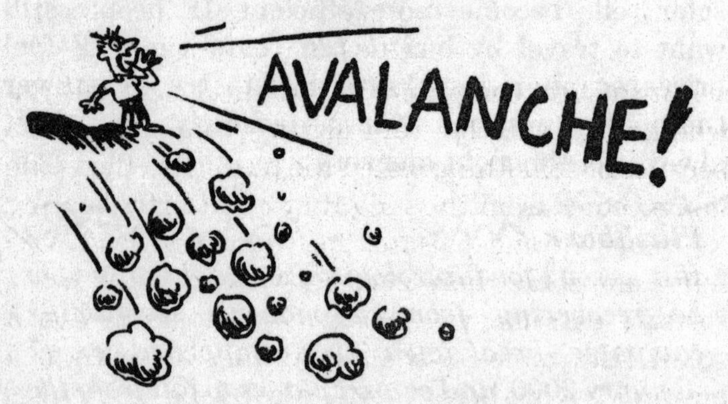


And it's all your fault! With one little stone! But not even you could have said in advance which stone it would be – even though you rolled it!

Good question. But think about the weather. Easy to predict – but only for a while. If it's raining 10 km to the west of you and the wind is blowing eastwards at 10 km an hour, it's easy to predict what might be happening in an hour or so...

But the best computers in the world can't tell you whether it will be raining in a month. That's because of something called the butterfly effect. The name comes from the idea that a butterfly beating its wings in one part of the world can lead to a hurricane somewhere else. Hurricanes – and other sorts of extreme weather too – can start with a small disturbance of the air, perhaps as small as a butterfly's wing-beat.

The thing is, many big things – avalanches, storms, fires that wipe out whole forests – have almost unnoticeably small starting-points: a pebble, a breeze, a spark. If conditions are exactly right, almost *any* pebble, breeze, or spark can do the trick (just like, if someone's in a really bad mood, even a tiny little tease can make them blow up unpredictably).

In each case, once the small event has happened, its effects grow and grow. It's typical of these sorts of things that, even *after* the big event takes place, it's normally next to impossible to say what tiny thing set it off – so it's not surprising that it's quite impossible to identify the tiny event *before* the big one happens. Which is why the big event is unpredictable.

The UK Meteorological Office can predict tomorrow's weather with 87 per cent accuracy. Sounds quite impressive? Well, maybe, but then again anyone at all can predict the weather tomorrow with 77 per cent accuracy, simply by assuming that tomorrow's weather will be more or less like today's. Achieving that extra 10 per cent has taken centuries of research, tonnes of phenomenally powerful computers, billions of measurements and millions of pounds.

Unfortunately, chaotic systems like this are very common, and predictions about them are always going to be a bit pants. Much to the annoyance of futurologists.

***Flashback***

*In October 1987, a TV weather forecaster said he'd heard a rumour that there was a hurricane on its way to England the next day. "Don't worry," he said, "there isn't." The next day...*

Luckily, not all systems are chaotic, but there is another problem with forecasting: to get things right, you have to not only predict *if* something will happen, but *when*...

## Tricky predicting 2: rising curves

Predicting when something will happen is tricky since, as time goes on, the rate of progress increases: many things change more quickly each year. Like transport, for instance. Thousands of years ago, any sort of progress was incredibly slow – it took centuries to invent saddles and bridles for horses, and more centuries to perfect them.

So, for someone living long ago, it must have seemed that nothing would ever improve. In fact, an ancient Roman engineer called Sextus Julius Frontinus even said in AD 98:

But in, say, 1903, no one on Earth – let alone an engineer – would have said any such thing. New inventions were in the news every few months. That year, an American called Orville Wright struggled into the air in the first ever powered heavier-than-air flying machine.

From then on, there was a frenzy of airborne invention in which speed, distance, height and flight-duration records were broken over and over again, until, less than 70 years afterwards, in 1969, another American left the Earth's surface – on his way to the Moon. (Actually, getting to the Moon was something science-fiction writers had been predicting for centuries, though they all got the method of getting there completely wrong.)

To see that the rate of progress increases, just skim through any history of technology, or science, or discovery, or invention, or just about anything else – there will probably be more pages covering the last 200 years than the previous 2,000. In fact, there were more inventions in the 20th century than in all the previous 19 centuries put together!

But *why* was the rate of progress so slow in the past? There are many reasons, including:

• for many centuries, in most countries, the Church was resistant to change and stopped it when it could.

• until a few centuries ago, communication over long distances was very difficult, so good ideas didn't spread.

• most people worked in manual jobs most of the time, so they had no time to develop new things.

• most people were poor so there wasn't much of a market for new inventions.

In Western Europe, most people were illiterate until the 16th century, so they couldn't record any new ideas they came up with before then. It wasn't until the 17th century that science really got going and only in the 18th century was it used to solve many practical problems. Universities and industry only started to organize and fund research properly in the 19th century, and it wasn't until the 20th century that large numbers of people began to be highly educated and then paid to develop new things.

These days, huge teams of people are trained and employed by companies and universities and governments to come up with new inventions, and anything useful is developed and sold as quickly as possible. People know that money can be made from new discoveries, and the most successful countries are well organized, with good communications and educational systems, and with money to spend on research. So now, lots of people are trying to move the world ahead as fast as they can.

Predicting exactly what the future will be like is impossible ... but don't stop reading. There are several certainties and piles of probables ahead: exploring the future is like walking through a misty city – some things, especially close ones, are clear and well defined, while others loom vaguely in the distance, and you won't know for sure what they are until you're almost on top of them.

Let's start close to home – in fact, let's have a look inside your future bedroom (so you'd better have tidied it up...)

# THE WORLD IN YOUR ROOM

If you're reading this in your bedroom, have a look round. If you're lucky, you'll see books and magazines, a mobile, a PC with email and Internet access, a TV, radio, various remote controls, maybe a few postcards and photos of your mates – in other words, your room is stuffed to busting with communication devices.

Over the last few centuries, a big chunk of the inventions people have come up with have been related in some way to communication, from posting letters to sending texts. Communicating is something that people have always wanted to do. You were trying to do it as soon as you were born and well before you'd learned how (and very irritating for your parents it was too). You'll probably spend the rest of your life talking, phoning, writing, emailing and texting thousands of people.

Our keenness to communicate means that, in a few years, your bedroom might look something like this:

THOUGHT-
CONTROLLED
LIGHT
REWRITABLE
BOOK
SUPER-MOBILE
PHONE
MIND-READING
BED/CHAIR

ADVANCED TV/DVD/COMPUTER SYSTEM (CONTROLLING WALLPAPER)
PC
SMART WALLPAPER
VIRTUAL-REALITY SYSTEM
YOUR VIRTUAL FRIEND
VR
CARPET THAT CARES

**1. Super-mobile phones**

Every so often in your future bedroom, your mobile will beep for attention and then tell you that your favourite band is about to start their gig. You'll send a quick text to those of your friends who like that band (your mobile will know which friends these are), and you'll be able to see and hear their performance – also on your mobile, which will record the best bits for later, too.

Today, almost everyone who can afford a mobile has got one, so, to go on selling them, the manufacturers have to keep coming up with new gizmos. It seems certain that soon mobile phones will be able to access the web at broadband speeds, transmit high-quality live-video images with stereo sound, and link up easily with PCs to download files. They'll have built-in satellite TV systems too, and will even lock on to satellite signals so they can guide you home if you get lost.

The big problem with these phones might be that with so many functions, they'd have to be as big as a book to hold the keyboard.

So they'll need to recognize speech. Machines that can do this have been around a long time, but they aren't all that good, mainly because of the way we run our words together and pronounce the same words differently at different times. So perhaps we'll start to speak in a way that's easy for the phone to cope with. Like this:

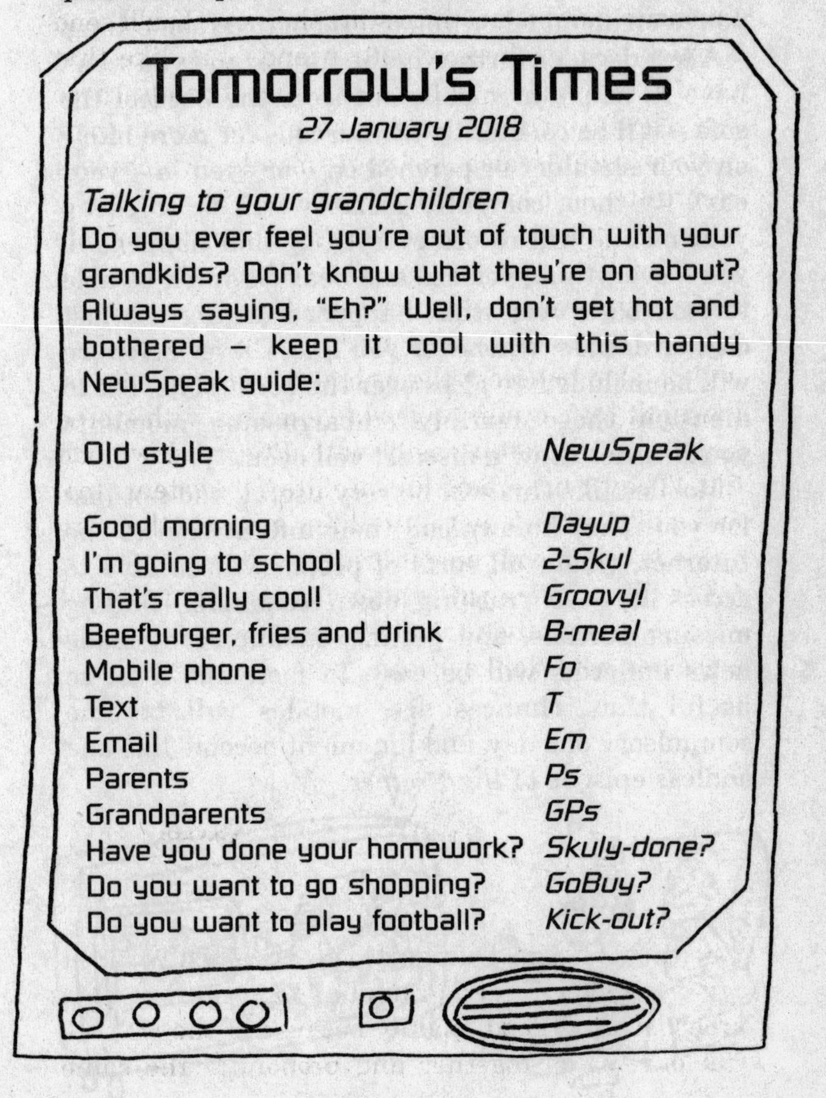

# Tomorrow's Times

*27 January 2018*

*Talking to your grandchildren*

Do you ever feel you're out of touch with your grandkids? Don't know what they're on about? Always saying, "Eh?" Well, don't get hot and bothered – keep it cool with this handy NewSpeak guide:

| Old style | *NewSpeak* |
| --- | --- |
| Good morning | *Dayup* |
| I'm going to school | *2-Skul* |
| That's really cool! | *Groovy!* |
| Beefburger, fries and drink | *B-meal* |
| Mobile phone | *Fo* |
| Text | *T* |
| Email | *Em* |
| Parents | *Ps* |
| Grandparents | *GPs* |
| Have you done your homework? | *Skuly-done?* |
| Do you want to go shopping? | *GoBuy?* |
| Do you want to play football? | *Kick-out?* |

In the future, mobiles are also likely to use built-in cameras to detect nods and shakes of your head and even to lip-read, to help them understand what you're on about when you tell them to do something.

A few decades further in the future, and you won't have to fish your mobile out from the back of the sofa – it'll be constantly at your side (or more likely on your shoulder or perched on – or even in – your ear). By then, computer memory will be so cheap your mobile will record everything that happens to you – everything you see and hear. So you'll be able to look back over what happened during the last day, or decade: whenever you like. Clever software will be included, to gloss over the boring bits, not to mention those terribly embarrassing moments you'd rather draw a discreet veil over.

Mobiles like this will be very useful, and not just for you. They'll download their information to the Internet, where all sorts of people will be able to access it – so tracking down criminals, finding missing persons, and getting instant ready-made news bulletins will be easy. In fact, they'll be so useful that, chances are, mobiles will become compulsory one day, and life might become like one endless episode of *Big Brother*.

**2. Thought-controlled lights**

These sound very science fictionish, but actually the way they'll work isn't all that complicated:

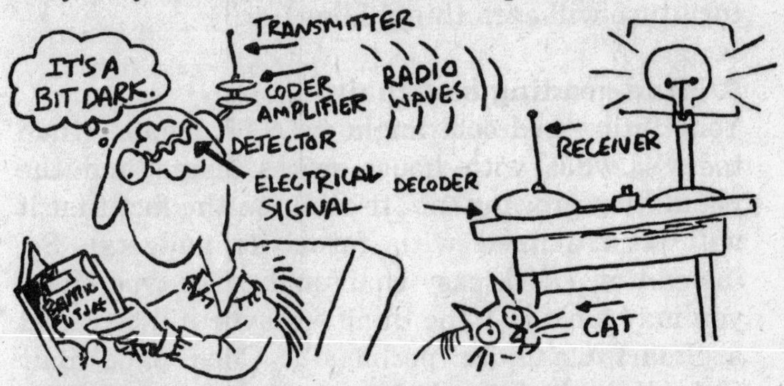


Imagine a whole world of thought-controlled gadgets that will work just like this:

As well as inventions that respond to instructions that we deliberately "think" at them, there will be some that sense our mood. Some of your bedroom furniture will even think! Like...

### 3. Mind-reading bed/chair

Your future bedroom might be a bit smaller than today's, what with house prices rising and the population growing (not to mention the fact that it will be crammed with futuristic gadgets). So, instead of a bed, easy chair and office-type chair, you may have just one thing – maybe it'll be called a Smart Chair, or perhaps a Ched or a Bair (actually, to be brutally honest, it might be called a Thunker for all I know – predicting what it's called is harder than predicting how it works). Anyway, imagine you've just finished your homework and it's time to listen to some music. Even as you think so, your "Ched" softens and reclines. Music comes out of it until you start to get sleepy, and the music softens and dies as the Ched gets wider and flatter and softer. It warms up a little, folds itself gently around you and you fall peacefully asleep...

How does it work? Well, your brain produces regular patterns of electricity all the time, which depend on how you feel – these patterns change when you're alert, tired, or asleep. Cheds will have built-in detectors that will pick up and recognize these patterns. When your Ched notices that you're sleepy, it will turn into a bed, and when you're ready for homework, it will be too. When you're ready to get up, the Ched will be able to straighten gradually into a column – and then fold itself neatly away until you need it again.

Your Ched will have to do more than just respond to your brain waves though – otherwise, every time you close your eyes it'll turn into a bed. That's why it will have to "think" – to decide whether you really want to sleep, work, relax, or get up, based on the time, what you're doing, your usual pattern of behaviour and all sorts of other things.

**4. Carpet that cares**

This is a bit like your Ched in that it will change to suit you, but it will react to physical signals rather than thoughts – it will be snuggly and warm on a cold winter's morning, smooth and cool on a June afternoon. It will also solve that awful problem: do you let your parents into your room to clean it, do it yourself, or let it get dirty? This carpet will keep *itself* clean – and the rest of the room too – by absorbing dust from the air. All this could be done by a network of narrow tubes down which cool or warm air is blown, or dust is sucked. The carpet will also act as a burglar alarm if someone steps on it when you've told it you're out. Perhaps carpets like this could even trap burglars like flies in a web, by squirting a network of sticky threads over them that harden in the air.

**5. Virtual Reality system**

Virtual Reality (VR) involves a computer producing sounds, images and physical sensations so realistic that they can convince us that they're real. It's not as easy as it seems, because what we sense depends on how we move. Also, even the best VR systems around today don't generate smells or tastes, and physical sensations are limited to a few prods and presses on the inside surface of a glove you wear, or some jerks and wobbles of your chair. The easiest bit of a VR system to get to work is the audio system – stereo headphones are all you need, and they were around even before your parents were your age, practically for ever, in other words. Getting a realistic picture isn't too difficult either – for a three-dimensional effect, all you need is two tiny TV screens that show slightly different views, one for each eye.

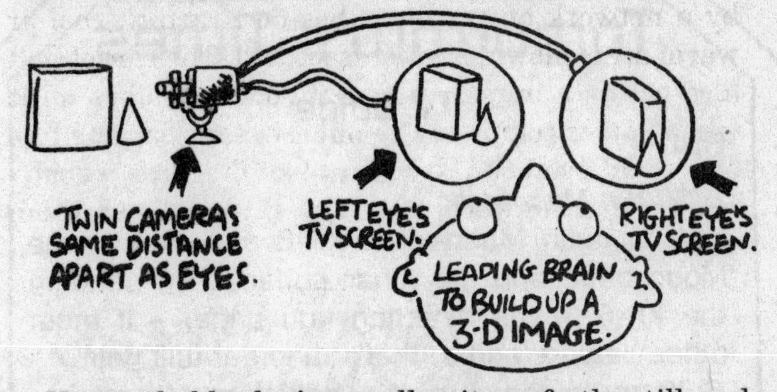


You probably don't usually sit perfectly still and stare in the same direction (except when there's something really excellent on the telly, of course). If you did, VR would be a doddle. What is tricky is making the images change realistically as you move. To cope with this, future VR systems will be able to detect every move you make and change the view to match.

Of course, when thought technology takes off, all this equipment will seem as outdated as a suit of armour. Just a little chip attached to your head – or surgically implanted into it – might do it all, feeding signals directly to the parts of the brain you use for seeing, hearing, touching, tasting and smelling.

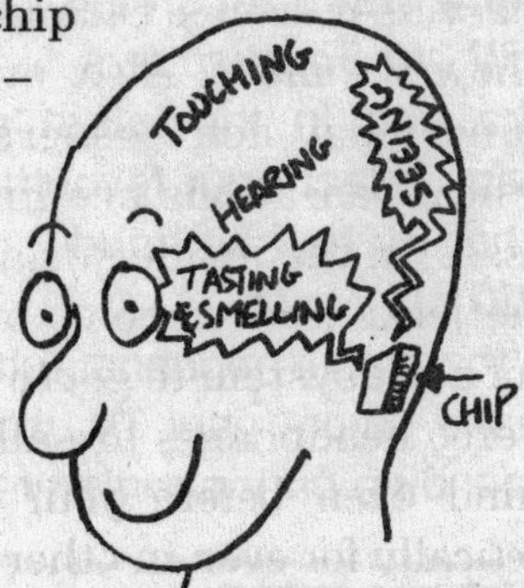

Once convenient, convincing VR systems are available, watching TV will be a *lot* more exciting:

# Tomorrow's Times

## TV Guide

BBC 7

*6:00 pm Moonwalk*
Link up with Moon-robot XR-6 and explore the Moon base and the lunar surface. Try sending the XR-6 in the direction you prefer – if most other viewers agree, that's where it will go!

*6:30 pm In search of the Loch Ness Monster*
Join the latest search for Nessie. (But unless you're feeling tough, remember to switch off your VR temperature-pads: that water's going to be cold!)

*7:00 pm Sportsnight*
In a special edition, take part in the 1966 World Cup: find out how your foot feels when it kicks the ball, hear the crowd cheer as you score, see the players all around you. (For this edition, colour and extra detail have been added to the original 1966 recording.)

*8:30 pm Southenders*
Take part in the latest episode of today's top soap: select your favourite character and be him or her for half an hour!

*9:00 pm News*
Be there as it happens, where it happens. (Parents please note – your TV will edit out some scenes, depending on the registered age of the viewer.)

There'll be plenty of adverts on TV, too. If you like the sound of whatever they're offering, you'll be able to ask them questions about it and, if you're still keen, order whatever it is there and then. If the advert is for music or a film or game, the TV will download it instantly (and take the money out of your bank account, of course). If you've bought something else, you'll either be able to have it delivered or, to save money, it will be sent to a local collection point – like a petrol station – for you to pick up.

### 6. Rewritable books

In your futuristic bedroom, you might only have one book. At the press of a button – or a spoken word from you – its pages will change from a comic to a history book (when it's time to do your homework), and then maybe to a TV guide, A to Z, or the latest title in "The Knowledge" series, depending on what sort of an evening you have in mind. Rewritable books like this will look like ordinary books, but with thicker, glossier pages. Each page will have thousands of tiny spheres embedded in it. The spheres will be white on top and black underneath. When the book receives a computer file of data, some spheres will turn over, making black dots appear in groups, forming letters and pictures.

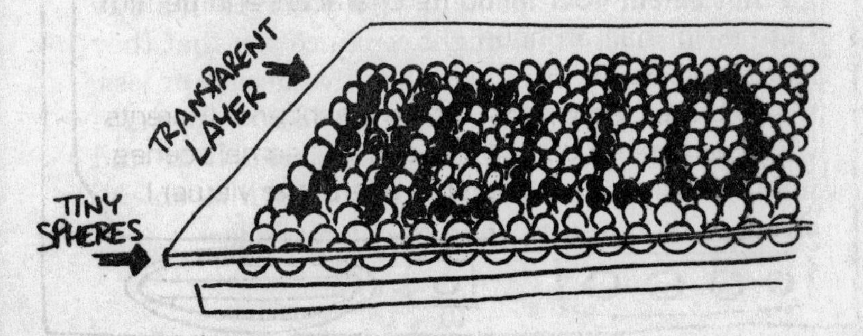

**7. Your virtual friend**

Have you ever got tired of your friends and wished you could swap them for better ones? Well, one day, you'll be able to. Imagine you're looking for a new friend on the Internet. You might want someone who:

Plays volleyball and football
Likes Egyptology
Eats fruit gums
Tells ghost stories
Hates geography
Doesn't pick their nose

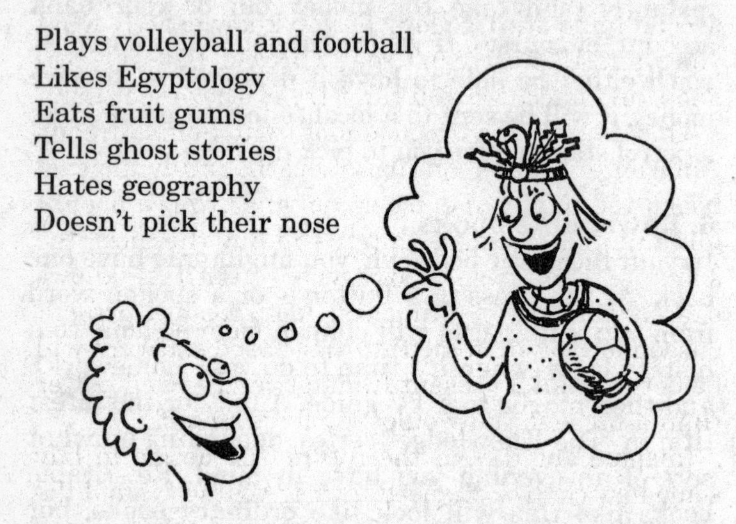

The system could then look through its register of all the people in the world it knows about, and offer you a likely new friend. Or, if there's no one suitable, it could make one for you! There are plenty of primitive versions of such friends – called Chatbots – on the Internet already. At the moment all they can do is respond to what you type in a way that, for a short time, might convince you that they are a real person. It's likely that, in a decade or less, they will be very much more realistic – perhaps with real-looking faces, voices you can hear and intelligence and emotions, too. And you'll be able to speak to them rather than typing messages.

## Cybershopping

What do you use the Internet for? Shopping? In that case, you'll already know that buying DVDs, books and CDs on line is far easier (and cheaper) than actually going to the shops, especially for second-hand stuff, so long as you know exactly what you want. But you can't really browse like in a real shop, and of course you can't try clothes on either.

This is where virtual shops will help. Already Amazon and other on-line shops helpfully suggest books you might like, based on what you've bought already, and the more things you buy the more the software can learn about you – until it knows exactly the sort of thing you like. Soon, a present chosen for you by some Internet-based software will be better than a present from a friend – even better than a present you would buy for yourself.

Imagine one day in the future you decide to buy some new clothes. No need to drag yourself round the shops in the rain, missing buses and wishing you hadn't worn those socks with the holes in. Just log on and activate your "avatar" – a virtual "you" who knows your measurements, your style and your budget.

Browse the on-line catalogues of the top shops and, when you see a jacket you fancy, your avatar will show you just how you'll look wearing it. Maybe you want some shoes in the same colour? It'll look around until it finds them – making sure they're real leather, if it knows that's what you like. Then it'll tell you the price – and if that sounds a bit steep, it will check out all the shops in the whole world to find the very best deal. Still too pricey? Then it'll look through all the jackets and shoes you *can* afford until it finds something similar. Decide you can't afford any of the shoes? It'll remind you which of your own shoes are most like the new ones, and show you how you'll look with the new jacket and those old shoes (automatically making them look a bit worn out, based on their age). If, after all that, you decide you don't actually *need* a new jacket, your avatar won't mind a bit – unlike a real friend you've dragged round the shops all morning. In fact, with friends like virtual ones, who needs people?

## Trends in trendiness

The clothes you get your avatar to shop for won't be quite like today's – imagine something that you could wear in any weather, that you could set to whatever colour you like, that would never need cleaning, and that could tell you exactly where you are in the world. Something like this...

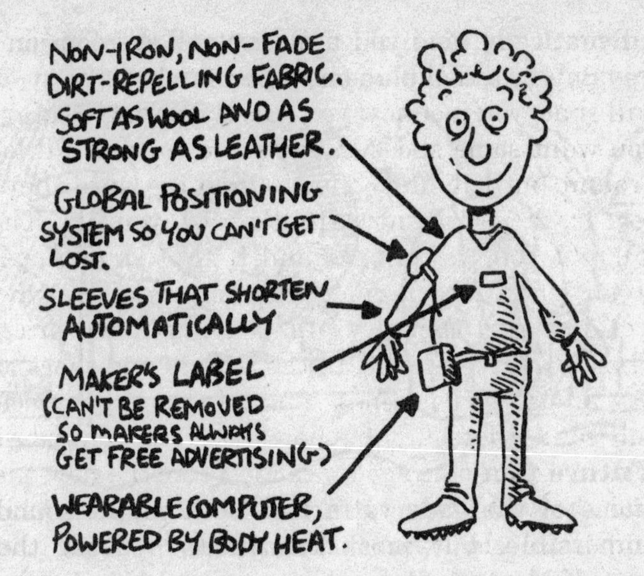


**8. Smart wallpaper**

Do you ever think your PC screen is a bit small? Fancy a change of wallpaper? Decide your room is a bit dark on a winter's day? Wish there was an IMAX* cinema round the corner? Well, smart wallpaper will solve all those problems in one go – although it won't really be paper. It will be made of several flat screens, like the ones you can get already for TVs and computers, but even thinner, bendy and much bigger. You'll be able to show on them all the things you can on a TV or computer screen – rolling clouds, jungle scenery, your favourite TV show, pop video, satellite picture or website. Or, if you prefer, nice flowery wallpaper or posters. You'll also be able to set smart wallpaper to

* A system that uses a screen so big it more or less fills your whole field of view.

automatically give you a sunny yellow room on a grey day, or a cool blue one when it's hot.

**Future fact**

Some of the gadgets in this book might sound impossible, but most inventions – from the grandfather clock to the record player to the phone – go through six stages:

**9. The Thinkernet**

The Internet has got steadily more popular since it was invented, and many people spend hours on it every day. Maybe one day we will get completely dependent on it:

Whether or not things go that scarily far, the Internet itself is likely to undergo some weird changes. VR systems, avatars, Chatbots, weather-forecasting software, speech-recognizers and anti-virus software are all, at least a bit, "intelligent" –

that is, they act in a way that we might call intelligent if a person did the same. All contain programs called "adaptive algorithms" that learn and evolve.

So, since parts of the Internet are growing more intelligent, could the whole system start to think? It might happen gradually – you may hardly notice as it starts to suggest books and pop songs that you really like, makes your emails wittier, writes your homework for you. Then you may find it suggesting holidays, friends, jobs... Some people are likely to end up trusting the Internet more than they do other people – already a lot of people who use Internet medical advice and counselling services find they feel more comfortable sharing their problems with a machine than a person. So, in a few years, you might find yourself asking the Internet what subjects to study or how to deal with your parents.

***Flashback***

*In 1943, the head of IBM – one of the world's biggest computer companies – said, "I think there is a world market for maybe five computers."*

**Deadweb?**

Will the Internet be more important in the future? You'd think so, considering how handy it is for everything from homework to email. But it's just possible that it won't: every year thousands of new computer viruses are created, and every year thousands of fixes are developed. But, just as in human history there have occasionally been plagues that have ended whole civilizations, we might one day face a computer virus so unstoppable that the Internet will be completely destroyed – which might cause chaos. Even then, though, it's hard to imagine that it won't be mended eventually.

The Internet could even become intelligent overnight. People don't call computer viruses that for nothing – they really are like primitive aggressive life forms, that change the way the things they infect function. By tapping into the mind-blowing amount of information on the Internet, a virus not much more advanced than the ones we hear about every month could transform the whole system – into a vast brain...

# SCHOOL'S OUT

If you were hoping school might disappear in a few years, you probably won't want to read this chapter. Because school is about learning to deal with people as well as with facts and figures, going to school is going to stay around for a while at least.

But one thing that is likely to change in a few decades is teaching. Though teachers will still be real people you can see, they may not actually be there! Instead, your classroom might be inhabited – or maybe haunted is a better word – by a 3D-image of a person who is actually in a studio 100 km away. The system might work like this:

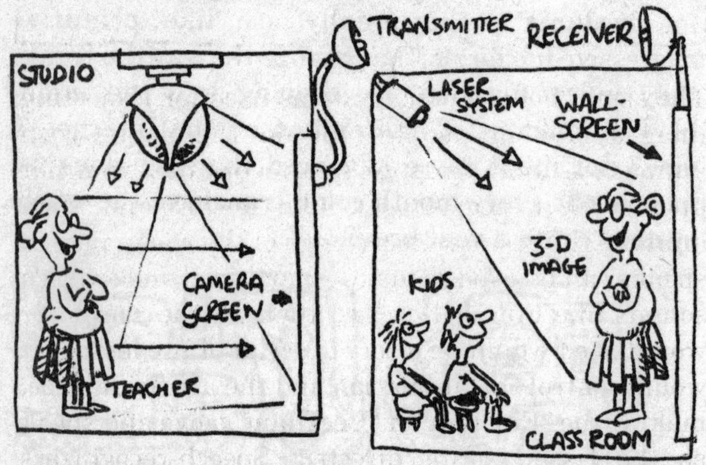


What's the point? Well, for one thing, it would mean one teacher could run several classes at once, and would allow people in small, remote schools to study any subject without the school worrying about finding a local teacher who specializes in it.

That's just the start. How about learning physics from Einstein, playing football with Beckham, taking piano lessons from Beethoven, or writing plays with Shakespeare?

The same "holographic" systems used for projecting images of real people can do the same with animations, and computers can work out from flat photos what people look like in 3D and then animate the results. Recordings of the way a person speaks can be used to make an artificial voice which sounds like him or her, and then all the computer would need would be a sort of script of the lesson. It would control the animation and the artificial voice, making the "Einstein" or "Beckham" move and speak as the lesson script directed. Speech-recognizers could detect and analyse questions from the class, and feed them to what is called an "expert system". This is a type of program that contains all sorts of information about a subject – like physics – and that can arrange the information in various ways, depending on the question it is asked. So, if "Einstein" was in the middle of explaining how a prism works and you said, "What's a prism?", the teaching program would interrupt the script, look up the word in its expert system, construct an answer-sentence, and feed it to the Einstein animation, which would then pass it on to the class.

All this *could* be done more simply with a VR system, but then you wouldn't be able to share a class with other people. But some days each week probably will be spent at home, with a VR system. And they'll be used full-time for pupils who are ill, and maybe for space travellers.

## Webwatchers

One thing that might be a problem with virtually going to school is that it will be a lot easier to virtually skive off! With a nice helpful virtual friend, who would know? (And it might not just be pupils that do this – teachers could, too.) There might have to be virtual truancy inspectors – special programs designed to spot the difference between fake humans and real ones – patrolling the Internet like virus-detecting programs and web-search programs do now.

***Flashback***

*In the 1950s, it was thought that, simply by playing tapes of lectures and lessons to people while they slept, people could learn things overnight, so they wouldn't have to go to school. Sadly, not only do people not learn much like this, they don't sleep too well either.*

Another thing that's likely to change is that there will be people of many different ages in the same classes – people will move up to the next "year" as soon as they've learned enough, so they might end up leaving university at 14. But the classes they take won't be the same as today's – imagine a school week like this one...

WEDNESDAY
FIRST AID: ON ROBOTIC DUMMY.
OUCH!
PHYSICS: MODELLING STARS.
MASS OF SUN SET TOO HIGH. SOLAR SYSTEM DESTROYED!
HOME ECONOMICS: GM FOODS.
MIX ANTI-FLU BANANAS WITH STONELESS PEACHES, WASP-REPELLING RASPBERRIES, BLUE ORANGES AND TOOTH-CLEANING APPLES.
THURSDAY
PE: HUMANS UNITED V. ROBOT WANDERERS.
YESS!
JAPANESE: VIA INTERNET LINK WITH TOKYO.

***Flashback***

*In the 1960s, when everyone was just getting really excited about computers, it was thought that soon teachers would be replaced by learning machines – which looked more like cash-registers than PCs and would ask the student a huge series of questions – like one enormous multiple-choice exam.*

## Faster than thought

As technology advances still further, the way in which we learn things may change completely. What is learning anyway? It's a process in which information that we receive through our senses is fed to the brain in the form of tiny electrical signals.

Physical changes then take place in the brain, as tiny fibres of brain tissue grow and connect up with each other, forming memory patterns. (This is a little bit like the way videotape records sounds and pictures by arranging tiny magnets in patterns.) If the information is repeated, or you make an effort to memorize it, these memory patterns strengthen and remain in the brain – sometimes for the rest of your life.

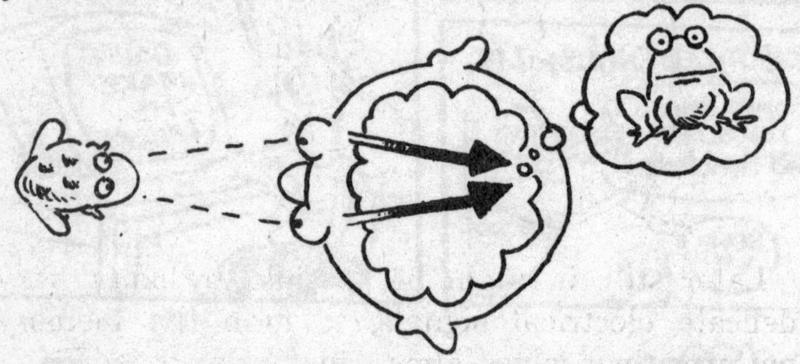

Already, thanks to VR, it's possible to supply the eyes and ears with what seem to be sights and sounds from the real world, but which are actually formed on small TV screens and loudspeakers.

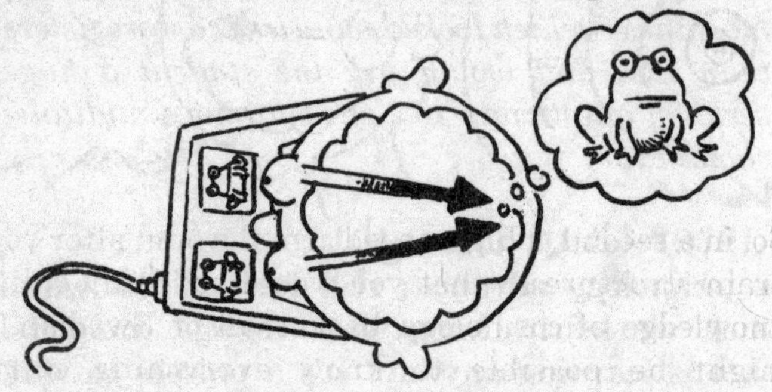

One day, it will be possible to bypass the eyes and ears completely and supply the brain with artificial signals which are just like those the senses generate. Then you'd have the experience of seeing and hearing things which aren't really there (and feeling, smelling and tasting them too – all things which are very tricky to do using VR).

Later still, it might be possible, by using very delicate electrical signals, to form the memory patterns themselves, almost instantly.

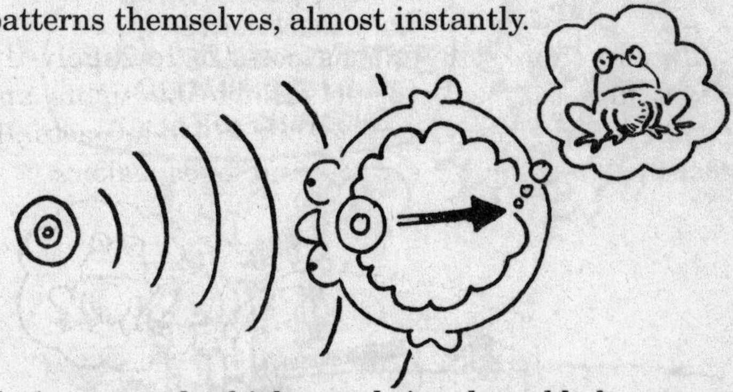

So, in a second, a high-speed signal would alter your brain structure so that you would suddenly gain a knowledge of cosmology, basketball or Swedish. It might be possible to know everything worth knowing! On the other hand, though huge, the capacity of the human brain is not limitless, so you might run out of memory space to store all those memories. This might be a very weird feeling. Most likely, though, it will just mean that you forget more and more seldom-used information as the brain restructures itself to take on new material.

One great thing about future education is that you'll be able to find out about absolutely anything, in any way you like: Mars, dinosaurs, robots, time-travel, archaeology. All that's needed is some slightly smarter software than we have now to search the Internet, check what it finds there, and edit the information into whatever form you want: text, cartoons, animations or speech (which could even be spoken by your favourite robot).

# CYBERVILLE

Imagine going for a walk in the city where you live, in a hundred years' time...

Closing the door of your one-room flat behind you, you take the lift down from the 150th floor. Through the glass walls, you see the same pattern of streets your great-grandparents knew. There is a scattering of ancient buildings too – from the 17th to the 21st centuries – brightly spotlit for all to see. But around you, like tree trunks in a forest for giants, hundreds of enormous skyscrapers pierce the clouds. In the distance, you can just see the greyish sprawl of the East Reach, a mix of factories and slums that you've never visited.

Your lift sighs to a halt and the doors slide open. You pay a quick call on your great-grandparents on floor 89 – they don't go out much now they've turned 100. The security system lets you in – laser-scanning your eyes to double-check who you are – and, as you enter, a group of crab-like dust-bots scurry away to rinse themselves clean, and the television switches itself off. You chat to your great-grandparents while a servicer robot makes the tea.

Visit over, you take the lift to the ground floor. The foyer of your building is empty, but you're closely watched as you leave, and the building's computers signal the StreetNet system. It will track your progress from now on.

Like a giant wasp, a buzzing spybot flutters around you, trying to get a clear view of your face and a good sample of what you smell like. Satisfied, it swoops away, updating the StreetNet system with your latest position.

Outside, there's not much natural light, thanks to the vast shadows of the skyscrapers, but, as you make your way along a walkway, overhead lights sense your presence and switch on briefly as you pass. There is more light from huge video-adverts, which cover most of the skyscrapers.

A chill gust of wind wafts a strange mix of smells at you from the adverts across the street – fresh coffee, the latest perfume, sea air. It also blows a newspaper across your path – you glimpse a moving video clip of the cricket highlights playing on its front cover.

As you walk past the paper, a cat-sized robot scuttles out and snatches it up, its glittering solar panels spread out like the wings of an insect. A moment later, you see something moving in a shadowy corner – a bloated rat-like, dog-sized creature. It vanishes down a drain as you pass by.

You hurry into the tube station. The entrance scanner reads your ID card, debits the fare (in Euros) from your account, checks for weapons and drugs and greets you by name. As usual, there is a long queue for the tube, and no free seats.

The train accelerates down the tunnel, then races along the tube as it curves up into the morning sky.

## High rise

The way cities are developing is a success for futurology – skyscrapers were predicted decades before the first one was built in 1885. Futurologists realized that cities were bound to grow in size, but because land is limited, they would have to grow *up* as well as out. In 1926 there was a film called *Metropolis*, set in a 21st-century city looking very like Tokyo or New York does in the real 21st century. There are a few differences, though – in the film, the air is full of planes but, in the real world, very few aircraft are allowed in cities because of the risk of accidents. Also, New York isn't menaced by catastrophic floods or an evil shape-changing robot just now.

So, the future of cities is one of the easier things to predict. As populations grow, cities will too: they'll get bigger, with more complex systems, more criminals, more pollution and more vermin. But some things will change completely...

## A life in the sky

In a few decades, if you live in a city (and you probably will), you might be living upstairs – and not going out much. Skyscrapers will be a bit like villages were a few centuries ago – everything in walking distance and not many reasons to leave (especially considering the dangers that lurk outside). Your future home might look like this:

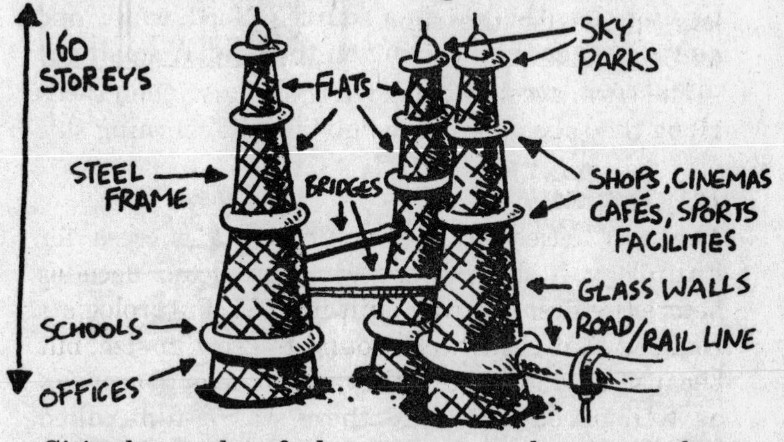


Cities have a lot of advantages over the country, but they have a big problem: they aren't *built* big, they *grow* big, which means transport, power, water, sewage and all other systems have to be constantly expanded. But they never quite catch up with what the city needs – and they always have to be more complex than systems planned and built just once would be.

## City-on-sea

One sort of city that is easy to grow, just by sticking new bits on the edges, is a floating one! The inhabitants could move it to somewhere warmer or cooler or prettier or more peaceful when they wanted to. The first ancestors of cities like this are floating about already – a few people already live permanently on giant cruise ships. They like being free to move round the world, not dependent on any one country. Perhaps the people who live in future cities will feel the same, and the cities will be like little countries of their own. In any case, they're likely to use the sea as a source of food, water and power, rather than relying on the land. A small one might look like this:

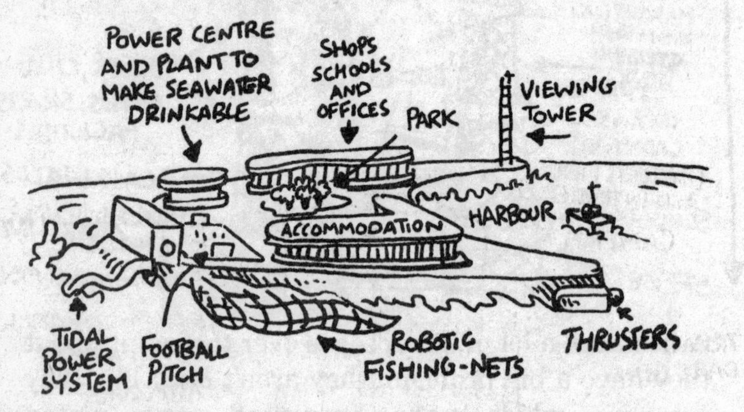


## StreetNet

One reason you might want to stay in your skyscraper is that everywhere else you go you'll be constantly watched by security cameras. Unlike today's, these will be so small you won't spot them. They'll also be intelligent – so they'll track you, pass on your details to the next camera once you're out of shot, and phone the police to protect you if you're in trouble (or to arrest you if you *make* trouble). You'll also be tracked by every door you go through and every thing you buy. And you'll have to carry a smart-card, which, together with all the other things it does, will tell the city security system where you are every minute of every day.

## Robotic rescue

If you do need rescuing – or arresting – it might not be by the police. Meet the cyberpatroller:

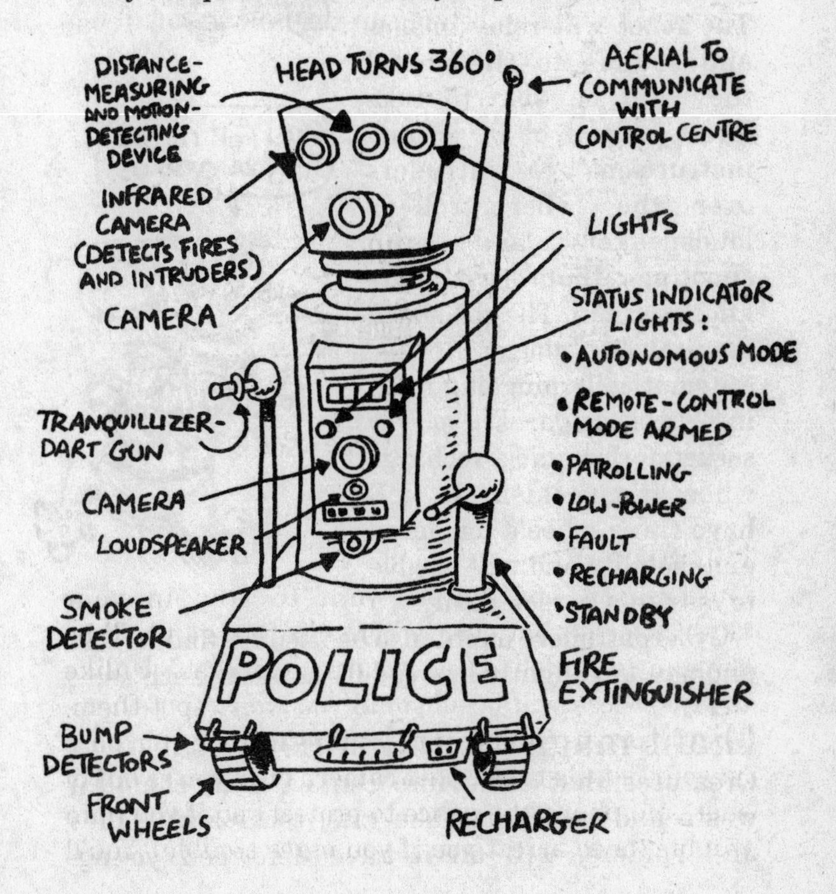

This type of security robot will be intelligent enough to patrol by itself, and will be able to detect smoke and fire. It will also automatically track moving objects. When it notices anything suspicious, it will alert human security guards at a control centre. The robot will relay images and sounds to them, and they will be able to take direct control of it, issuing instructions to intruders over the cyberpatroller's loudspeakers and even shooting them with its knockout gun. The robot will monitor its power levels, automatically plugging itself into the nearest power socket for a quick recharge when it's peckish. It will have three wheels for speed and mobility and will be able to outrun a person easily.

Cyberpatrollers might also be used for finding lost puppies and slightly less cuddly animals, such as...

## Giant maggots and super-rats

Creatures that come into contact with chemical waste and pesticides, like rats, cockroaches, flies and spiders, will often have deformed young.

Sometimes these young will have something that makes them tougher than their parents – they might be extra big, super fast, or exceptionally brainy or poisonous. In which case, they'll survive to breed and pass on what makes them special – so the dark places of cities a century ahead might be crawling with giant maggots, venomous spiders, poison-resistant cockroaches, super-fast scuttling centipedes and rats that think and scheme.

## Powertown

One thing cities will always need loads of is power. Tube trains, street lighting, heating, air-conditioning, communications systems, lifts and escalators – they all need oodles of the stuff. "Fossil fuels" like oil and coal are running out and make lots of pollution, so the cities of tomorrow will need something else. Until the 1970s, most people thought there was only one answer: nuclear power. When this was generated for the first time in the 1940s by breaking down deadly radioactive fuel to give lots of lovely energy – as well as, sadly, deadly radioactive waste – it seemed that it was the answer to everyone's problems. People even thought atomically produced electricity would be so cheap that it wouldn't be worth metering. The trouble is, radioactive waste has turned out to be such a problem that we're never likely to see the atomic cars, central-heating systems and passenger planes we were promised 50 years ago.

Luckily, there are other ways of making power – so rather than a city full of everything from atomic toasters to nuclear-powered tube trains, what we might have to look forward to is something a lot safer:

These systems work like this:

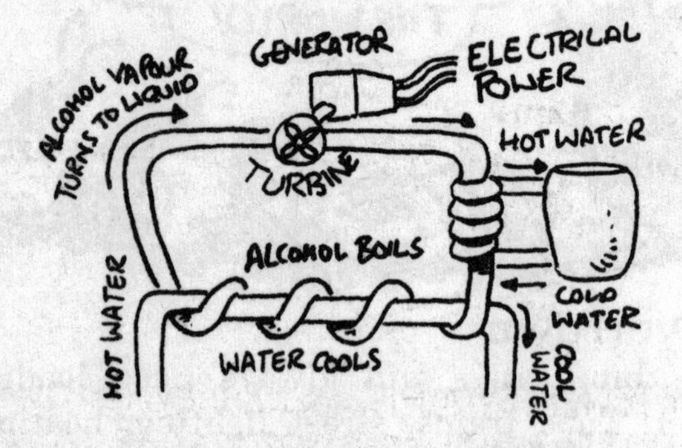


GEOTHERMAL SYSTEMS EXTRACT ENERGY FROM UNDERGROUND, WHERE IT'S ALWAYS HOT.

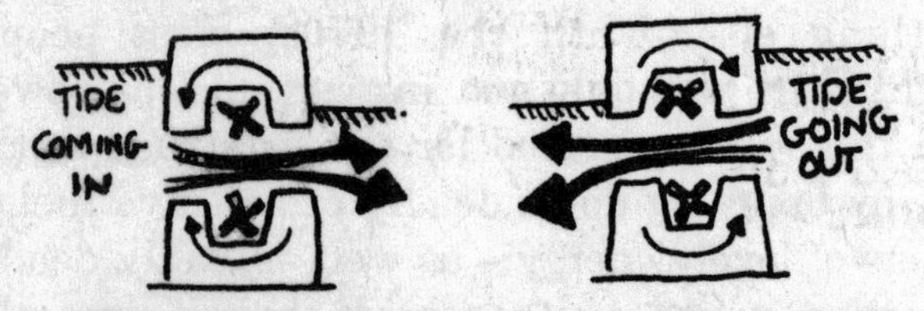


TIDAL POWER SYSTEMS USE THE VAST POWER OF THE OCEANS.

The great things about all these power sources is that they're inexhaustible and they're clean – that is, they don't generate chemical pollutants. There will still be plenty of pollution around in the future, though – probably more of the stuff than ever. The old fossil-fuel power stations and nuclear reactors may well continue alongside cleaner power sources, and there'll still be plenty of industry to pour pollution into the land, air and sea. Some countries will probably reduce pollution levels, but it's not likely that they *all* will. Noise- and light-pollution are likely to still be problems as well.

## Super-atomic

Another type of power will take a lot longer to develop than wind or wave power – nuclear fusion. Fusion reactors are different to the sort of reactors (called fission reactors) around today: instead of taking radioactive materials and breaking them apart, fusion reactors work by squeezing much smaller atoms together until slightly bigger ones form. In the process, loads of energy is released. There are some very handy things about atomic fusion – you can use water as fuel, it doesn't make tonnes of horrible, scary, poisonous waste and even if things go badly wrong, fusion reactors won't blow up, melt down, catch fire or poison half the country like today's reactors will – they'll just stop working. The big problem is that it's very difficult to squeeze the atoms hard enough to get them to combine – though this *can* be done already, at the moment it takes more energy than the atoms release. When fusion reactors get going, they'll probably produce most of the world's energy – but they'll probably always be too big to fit into cars or planes or toasters...

## Auto-city

As the centuries pass, and cities become more and more advanced, they will need less and less looking after as they become more and more automatic. There will be:

**Automatic cleaning systems:** when the city is quiet, robots will collect litter, then built-in water-jets will hose down windows and streets, and finally other robots equipped with steam-jets and scrapers will deal with any remaining problems, like those stubborn bits of chewing gum that get stuck to your trainers.

**Smart transport systems:** intelligent software will predict what people will want (school buses in the mornings, trains to the country on sunny days, tubes to the airport on Friday evenings...) and supply the right number of the right type of vehicle on the right route at the right time. When demand is predicted to be low, vehicles will be robotically cleaned and checked and repaired.

**Weather handling systems:** rainwater will be used for cleaning and cooling, the wind harvested by wind farms, and sunlight will be used to heat water and make electricity. Shades, mirrors and covers will open and close automatically to direct more natural light down to street level on dull days, or act as umbrellas on wet ones.

**Automatic repair systems:** built-in sensing devices will automatically call out maintenance robots to repair damaged bits of city, while cracked roads, walls and paths will repair themselves – like this:

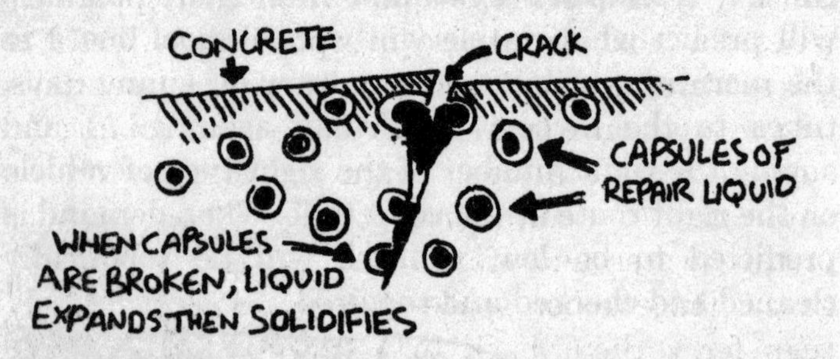


All of which means that, if visitors from space should arrive on Earth in a few centuries' time, they might discover that the main form of life here is a highly successful glass, concrete and steel creature well adapted to its surroundings, with the only problem being that it is overrun with parasites called people...

# TIMELINE OF TOMORROW 2: THE 22ND CENTURY

**2110** Many people travel in cars which can change colour and extend themselves to cope with extra passengers. But there are no drivers any more: computers choose the routes and guide the cars there – at 500 km an hour.

**2120** Global warming has raised sea levels by over a metre, flooding many coastal- and low-lying areas, including parts of London. Snow no longer falls in England.

**2130** There are over 13 billion people on Earth – more than twice the number in the early 21st century. Many of the people live in vast sprawling cities. In poor countries, overpopulation leads to water shortages and famines. There are now cities on the Moon and Mars and village-sized colonies in several space stations. There are also miners on asteroids, collecting metals, water and frozen gases. Huge robot space-tugs ferry them back to Earth and the space colonies. (The advantage of mining asteroids is that they have weak gravities, so it's much easier to lift things off them than off a moon or planet.)

**2140** The oceans are used for all sorts of things: metals are extracted from them, seaweed is farmed and whales are herded like cattle for their meat and milk. Almost all the work is done by underwater robots.

**2150** There is a lot more co-operation between countries, so big projects like space exploration and dealing with pollution are organized by the whole planet.

**2160** Thanks to huge solar mirrors in orbit and smart chemicals in the air that 'seed' clouds to make it rain, the weather is more or less under human control. (Which means weather forecasts get a lot better!)

**2180** Tiny robots called nanobots – too small to see – float in the air and destroy pollutants. Others swim through our bloodstreams, keeping our bodies clean from the inside and repairing damage. Yet others are like microscopic Lego blocks that can move themselves around and join together. Some of these build themselves into cameras, microphones, and weather stations, so the whole world is under observation, and privacy is a thing of the past.

**2190** Many people live on enormous space stations in orbit around the Earth and near the asteroid mines. The space stations are huge tubes, 40 km long and 10 km wide. People live on their inner surfaces, where there are houses, farms, lakes and parks. Gigantic shutters open and close over a 24-hour period, making artificial days and nights. The cylinders spin slowly, so that people "stick" to the inner surfaces like washing does to the inside of a spin-dryer. This feels just like gravity does on Earth. In fact, living in the stations is very like being on Earth – except that the horizon curves up instead of down and people who look straight up can see houses high overhead.

# SPEED MACHINES

However much you enjoy your future life high in the city sky, you'll probably want to go out sometimes. When you do, there'll be a whole fleet of speedy machines just waiting to sweep you off your feet.

Transport is one area of life where just about everyone wants progress. We want it to be:

And, unlike some other things, like houses or furniture, just about everyone wants vehicles to *look* newer, cooler, smoother, smarter – in other words, futuristic!

So it's safe to say that going places in the future will involve amazingly great-looking and high-tech machines. The only problem is, it seems impossible to make a vehicle faster *and* quieter *and* cheaper *and* smarter – so it's not easy to say *exactly* how vehicles will change. But the car of tomorrow might look something like this:

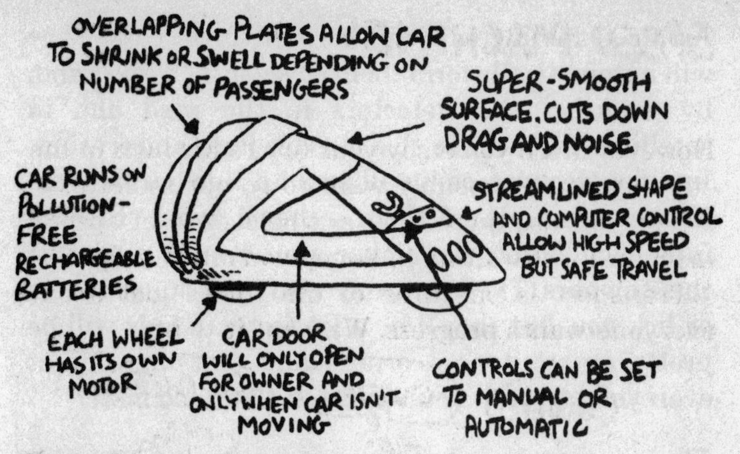


## Roads in the sky

Cities grow from towns, and towns have town-sized roads and railways. Since there's no space to widen these, skyways are one answer. These might be tubes that snake across the sky, transparent to avoid shadowing the streets below, sealed for safety and to keep the noise in. In a century, they might look like huge cobwebs draped across the cities of the world.

Artificial intelligence will be built in to cars. They will automatically form themselves into "herds", and, by working with detectors in the road and in satellites, they will be able to avoid jams and crashes. In a few decades, cars will be a bit like horses were before cars replaced them – they'll avoid crashing into each other, remember routes and recognize their owners. They probably won't eat sugar lumps or lick you, but they'll be a lot faster. Roads will be pretty smart, too – corners and crossings might even yell at you if you approach them too fast!

## Fun on wheels

As well as (or maybe instead of) push bikes, motorbikes and scooters, you'll soon be able to drive something that, even though it looks a little bit like a lawnmower, will be a lot more fun to use.

Having two wheels will make it cheap to build and run, easy to park in a small space and able to turn on the spot. At the moment, the problem with two-wheeled vehicles is that they tend to fall over at the most embarrassing possible moments, so this version will have something today's bikes and scooters don't – a "brain", that will

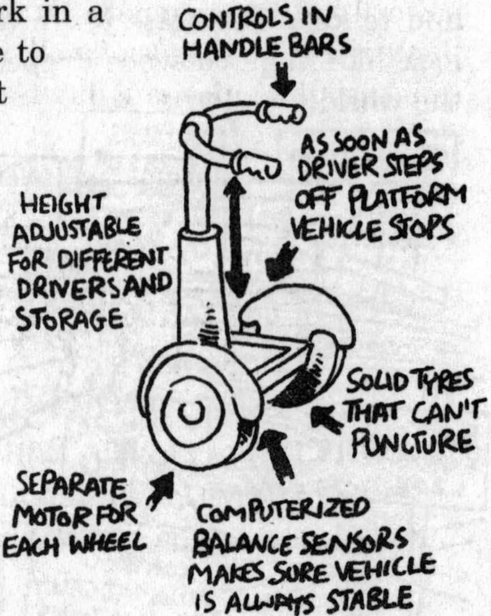

automatically adjust the wheels so that it never falls over. To steer, you'll just lean in the right direction and the brain will pick up the movement and turn the vehicle.

That's probably the sort of thing your grandchildren will use to go to school, or to visit their friends. But when they go to stay with their Aunt Nelly in Cornwall, they'll probably take a train – with no wheels. Wheels were a wheelly wonderful invention, but they are also a bit of a drag: they stick to the road (or rails), friction means their axles rub against their holders, the engines that power them are full of more wheels which also stick and rub and drag – and all this wastes energy, reduces speed, wears everything out and makes noise. So, future "maglev" (magnetic levitation) trains will have no wheels – instead, they will float a few millimetres above a track, held in place by powerful electromagnets. Other magnets will push them along, at speeds of well over 200 km per hour. And they'll be nice and quiet too.

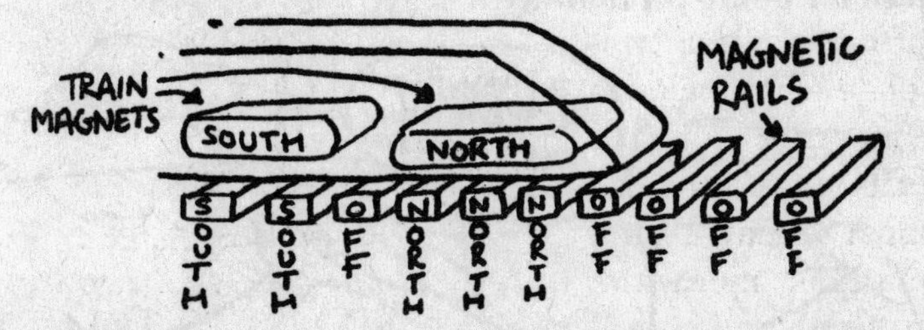


AS THE TRAIN MOVES, "RAILS" AUTOMATICALLY SWITCH FROM NORTH TO SOUTH, SO THEY ALWAYS REPEL WHICHEVER TRAIN MAGNET IS ABOVE THEM

## Future flight

In the 1940s, people thought that in future you'd just strap on a rocket pack and jet off to school. Or join your family for a spin in the flying car. Rocket packs and flying cars have both been built, but neither have caught on, for some very good reasons: it takes a lot more fuel and skill to fly than to drive, and it's a lot more dangerous if you crash. By the 1950s, people had decided that everyone would want planes of the future to be really fast, so they designed and built the world's first airliner that could fly faster than sound – Concorde, which took off in 1969. Unfortunately, it was the last such plane as well. Though people wanted speed, what they wanted more was quiet – and fast planes are noisy. That's why there are no Concordes in the air any more, and there aren't likely to be any more supersonic passenger planes until they can fly a lot higher and are a lot quieter on the way up and down.

There will probably be quite a mix of aircraft in the future. For a start, there will be huge passenger jets for going on holiday:

Then, for carrying goods, an ancient invention might make a comeback. They might be a bit slow, but airships have the wonderful energy-saving advantage that they need no power to stay up, because they are filled with gas that is lighter than air. They only need power to move along (and not much of that, if the wind's blowing their way).

## Higher than the sky

But some people will always need – or want – to go fast. If you're one of those people then, in a few decades, you might be flying higher than Mount Everest, higher than Concorde, on the very edge of space. Why? Air is made of little hard lumps called molecules, far too small to see. The front of anything that moves through the air bangs into these molecules, which slow the moving thing down. That's why it's harder to run in a big flappy coat – the coat increases the area that you need to drag through the air, so there are more molecules for you to bang into. The higher up you go, the fewer the molecules, so the less the air holds back moving things and the faster they can go.

Another advantage of high-altitude planes is that they're quiet – it's molecules that carry sound, so fewer molecules means less noise. High-altitude planes are also quieter because they're further away.

The only thing is, today's planes need air to fly – they suck it into the fronts of their engines and squirt it out the back, and their wings are held up by it, too. If you want to fly really high where the air is very thin, you'll need a rocket, so if you want to fly fast in the future, you'll use a rocket-plane.

Planes like this will fly 13 times faster than sound, at a height of about 100 km (six times faster and five times higher than Concorde). They'll be able to fly between London and New York in under an hour, or round the world in under three. Tickets on them won't be cheap, but there will be day returns – to anywhere on Earth.

# FUTURE CRIME

Some things never change. There has been crime ever since civilization began, and it might go on until civilization ends – certainly, it will be around for many years to come. But in the future, some crimes will be a lot more sophisticated than running off with someone's mobile. Luckily, so will crime fighting...

## Crimescene 2050

MEANWHILE...
IN AN EGYPTIAN MUSEUM
INSTRUCTIONS OBEYED.
NOTHING TO REPORT
POST
SECURITY
BUT SURVEILLANCE SATELLITES TRACK ALL ILLEGAL RADIO SIGNALS
19:10
GOTCHA!
ILLEGAL RADIO IMPULSES ORIGINATE SOMEWHERE IN CHURCH STREET BEFORE EACH THEFT.
MEANWHILE...
IN CHURCH STREET
SECURITY SYSTEM DISABLED. POST BOT INSTRUCTED TO REMOVE JEWEL.
TEE HEE HEE
THE CRIME TEAM SCAN THE AREA, DETECTING ELECTRICAL SIGNALS THAT LEAK FROM COMPUTER SCREENS IN EACH HOUSE AND REASSEMBLE THEM.
LOOK THE COMPUTER IN NUMBER 42!
COMMAND ACCEPTED. REMOVE JEWEL.

A LASER MICROPHONE MEASURES THE VIBRATIONS OF THE WINDOWPANE AND SMART SOFTWARE ANALYZES THEIR PATTERNS. THE SINGLE HEART BEAT AND BREATHING RHYTHM SHOW THAT THERE IS ONLY ONE PERSON IN THE ROOM. IT'S TIME FOR THE NET TO CLOSE...
SMASH
SECURITY ROBOT
WEB GUN
GOO GUN
LUBE GUN

Just fiction? But all these systems are already in use, even though we don't see much of them yet: non-lethal weapons, service robots, artificially intelligent crime-fighting systems, spy satellites, implanted chips to keep track of criminals. As for the crime: computer hacking is already a major problem all over the world, with banks and government computers being broken into every few days. Once radio-controlled robots are common, hacking into their systems might be just as easy.

One day we may be able to solve – or even prevent – all crimes: it could be one of the best things about the distant future. Which brings us very handily to the next chapter: put on your rocket-pack – we're going to the end of the Universe.

# TIMELINE OF TOMORROW 3: THE DISTANT FUTURE

Most parts of this book deal with the next few decades and centuries. But, compared to the span of future history, that period is very short. The vast and complex history of human civilization goes back about 10,000 years. A long time? But, assuming civilization survives at least until the Earth becomes uninhabitable in around 2,000 million years, that means we are only about 0.005 per cent of the way through the story! To put it another way, if you imagine the history of human civilization, from its primitive beginnings until the end of the world, shrunk into a single 24-hour period beginning at midnight, then the time right now is only about half a second past midnight.

This timeline is a journey through the vast stretches of time that lie ahead, up to and beyond the deaths of the Earth and Sun. Looking so far into the future is less like walking through a misty city, more like looking down a long, dark valley in the evening. The general shape is clear, but most details are lost in mist and shadow...

**2300** Nanobots are so advanced that they can break objects down into the atoms that they are made of and then build them up into other objects. This means they have the power to change anything into anything – rubbish into food, rags into clothes, or worse...

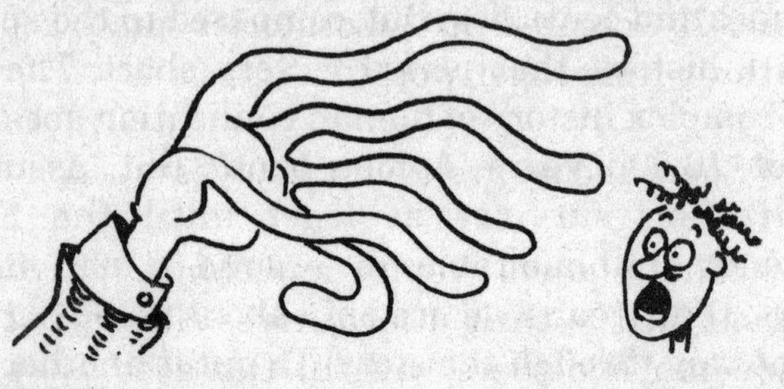

**2500** There are three main jobs: people who order robots around, astronauts (many of whom are asteroid miners) and artists (including writers and composers). There are over 100 times as many people alive as there are today, many living on the Moon, Mars and the moons of other planets in the solar system. With plenty of free time, people take part in all sorts of new sports, from space sailing to zero-gravity squash and robotic gladiatorial games. People rarely use written words any more – most writing is in the form of little pictures and diagrams called pictograms.

**3000** Astronauts have landed on planets going around other stars. Back home, Earth is a very different place. It is covered in cities made of skyscrapers hundreds of metres high and in vast fields of genetically engineered crops, harvested by robots. There are no natural environments left. Even the sea and the depths of the Earth are full of people, and most of today's animals and plants exist only in zoos. We share the Earth with all sorts of different intelligent creatures – clever robots, animals that have been modified until they can talk with people, new life forms that have been artificially created in laboratories and, possibly, creatures from other worlds.

**4000** Some people are over 1,000 years old.

**5000** The planets Venus and Mars have been "terraformed" – their atmospheres changed so that people can live there without the need for sealed buildings or spacesuits. The planet Mercury is the site of a vast solar power station, supplying energy to the Earth and other planets. It is inhabited entirely by robots. The asteroids supply the solar system with minerals, metals and water.

**10000** There are human colonies on many planets going round other stars, hundreds of thousands of billions of kilometres from Earth – so far away that radio messages take decades to travel between them. On some worlds, people have forgotten their ancestors ever came from Earth, and on others they've modified their bodies using robotic implants, genetic engineering or flesh-sculpting nanobots until they look like nothing we'd recognize as human.

**100000** Earth is in the grip of a new ice age: England and the rest of Northern Europe, as well as Canada, Russia, the northern United States, New Zealand and Southern South America, are all buried under many metres of ice and snow. Strange creatures, half animal, half machine, may roam the frozen wastes.

**1000000** By now, several kilometre-wide asteroids have smashed into the Earth, incredible volcanoes and massive earthquakes have destroyed whole cities and civilization has been demolished over and over again. Many world wars have wiped out most of the Earth's population. Each time the planet has been rebuilt, helped by the many other inhabited worlds in the solar system.

**2000000** There is an enormous metal sphere around the Sun, which catches all the light and heat it used to pour into space. All this power can now be used by people – most of it for space travel.

**10000000** Humans have spread through the entire Galaxy, following millennia of exploration, colonization and war. Many stars are entirely enclosed in spheres of metal and rock, with our descendants living on the inner surfaces. The dark outer surfaces might be covered by thick forests of fungus, full of strange creatures. But none are as strange as what we have become: with complete control over their bodies, the "people" of this period have whatever shape they like – so you may be the ancestor of many different creatures, some like mobile trees with eyes instead of leaves, others like enormous jellyfish drifting through interplanetary space.

**2000000000** The Sun, which has been gradually getting brighter for many millions of years, is now so hot that all the Earth's oceans have dried up.

**5000000000** The Sun starts to swell up, turning into a red giant star. The huge bursts of heat it produces strip the Earth's surface away. However, Mars is warmed up by the process and some of our descendants may survive there.

**6000000000** All the Sun's outer layers have boiled away into space and only a tiny dead (but still hot and bright) star called a white dwarf remains.

**15000000000** The white dwarf has cooled and faded and turned into a black dwarf: the solar system is dark and dead. The survivors of Earth have probably fled from the dying Sun and set up colonies on planets orbiting younger stars. Their descendants will be able to continue leap-frogging from one star to another for hundreds of thousands of billions of years.

**1000000000000000** By now, all over the Universe, Earth-like planets have drifted away from their suns, pulled away by the gravity of passing stars. As everlasting night falls, their atmospheres freeze solid.

**10000000000000000** Brown dwarfs drift through space. These are objects which are bigger than planets but not quite big enough to turn into stars. Here and there, brown dwarfs smash into each other and form small reddish stars called red dwarfs. Some of these stars have Earth-like planets orbiting them, the last to form anywhere in the Universe. Life will probably evolve on some – and perhaps ancient civilizations whose own suns have died may colonize them, too. If you time- and space-travelled to one of those final planets, the daylight might be red as sunset, and the night sky almost empty, with here and there a dim, red star or planet – red too – glowing feebly in the deep blackness.

**100000000000000000000** The last of the red dwarf stars burn out.

**10000000000000000000000000000000000000000**
The cold, dead remains of stars and planets have all been swallowed up by black holes, which are now the only type of star left in the Universe. Black holes have such strong gravity that not even light can escape from them, so they, and the Universe, are dark.

**10000000000000000000000000000000000000000000000000000000000000000000**. There is a final flicker of light in the Universe, as large numbers of black holes come to the ends of their lives and explode.

**10000000000000000000000000000000000000000000000000000000000000000000000000000000000000000000000000000** (The year ten thousand trillion, trillion, trillion, trillion, trillion, trillion, trillion, trillion.) With a final tremendous burst of light, the last and biggest black hole has exploded. With all the black holes gone, there are no stars or planets left anywhere in the Universe. There isn't a single grain of dust or wisp of gas anywhere, nor the faintest gleam of light or trace of warmth. Every atom that ever existed has long ago broken down into smaller particles, and those fragments are now the only things that exist. The Universe is completely and absolutely dead.

# HOW TO LIVE FOREVER

Even though living to the end of the Universe isn't an especially tempting prospect, what with all the exploding stars and freezing planets and everything, you may be thinking it's a pity you won't make it at least into the 22nd century to enjoy all the great things the future has in store – nipping off to Saturn for your Easter holidays, taking part in VR adventure games with your friends, playing football with your robot.

Well, maybe you will! For a start, if diseases continue to be wiped out in the future as they have been in the past, there's a good chance that you won't be killed off by anything in particular – just old age. If you're lucky and healthy, you could reach a hundred, no problem – especially since you'll be able to replace any bits of you that have stopped working in the meantime with shiny mechanical versions.

The reason you're not likely to make it much beyond a hundred is that in every cell of your body there is a sort of clock. Most cells live for quite short periods – days or weeks – and are then replaced. But your body clock keeps count of the number of times the cells are replaced and, after a certain number (which varies with the type of cell), the body stops replacing cells – and self-destructs.

There is a very good reason why this happens in nature – it's to make way for new generations of people. But it offers the chance of immortality (living indefinitely) because it means that, so far as we know, if the body clock could be reset, cells would go on replacing themselves for ever. In fact, there are lots of animals – like some types of lobster, shark and alligator – which never get old and go on living until something actually kills them. Their cells just replace themselves over and over again.

## New bodies

Body clocks are much more difficult to fiddle about with than the wind-up sort, mainly because they're about a zillion times smaller. To take control of them, scientists need to get even better at the science of genetics. There are several ways that human body clocks might be reset – changing the genes* of a baby before it is born would be easiest, but it might be possible to modify them even in a fully grown person, perhaps by the use of drugs. Scientists may even develop a type of virus which, once it infects someone, makes that person immortal.

Once they've mastered genetic control, scientists will be able not only to make cells immortal, but to make living copies (called clones) of you and me, too. Some clones have been made already – Dolly, the most famous sheep in the world, was a clone, born in 1997. But, though people can make clones already, they're not terribly good at it yet – so far, nearly all clones have major problems, like missing or misshapen limbs. Even Dolly, who seemed quite healthy and perky, died aged six – which is quite young for a sheep.

* Genes are the chemical instructions that tell the body how to grow – like the computerized instructions that tell factory robots how to build cars.

What's the point? Well, whilst cells might one day go on repairing themselves for ever, people will still have accidents or damage their bodies by smoking or drinking. But once someone has their own supply of body-copies, they could simply replace any of their damaged organs or limbs with fresh new ones. And if that killed off the clone, there would be plenty more. Sounds horrible? But people might do it, to save their lives. Would you?

Another idea is that spare body parts might be grown inside you. An extra kidney or two, a bundle of nerves or half a dozen spare eyeballs wouldn't take up much space and would be quite easy to move about inside the body to where they are needed when the old versions wear out.

Once this type of science is more advanced, people will be able to have completely new organs. If you like swimming, you could get some gills fitted. Or maybe you'd like eyes that can see in the dark? Or how about a nice pair of wings?

### The day of the cyborg

There are limitations to what we can do with genetics – for instance, it isn't possible to grow a radar, a laser or a radio communication system out of living tissue. For things like this, robotic parts could be used – they'd be quicker and perhaps easier to make, too. Half-human, half-machine creatures like this are called cybernetic organisms – cyborgs for short.

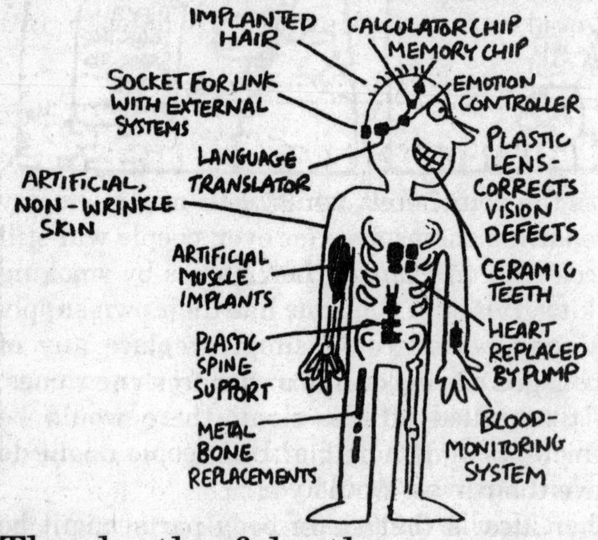


## The death of death

Once it's possible to live practically for ever, there will be no shortage of people wanting to try. For many years the technology will be so expensive that only the richest people will be able to afford the "eternity drugs" and robotic implants that could make them immortal. Once prices fall though, what will happen? As death becomes rarer, the world's population will grow rapidly and there will be all sorts of problems as a result. Maybe governments will restrict the use of eternity drugs. Or maybe, on the other hand, new babies will be banned to stop the world becoming overpopulated – so there might be no more new generations ever again. You might even be a member of the final generation.

But what would you do with your eternal life? Travel everywhere? Invent the ultimate sandwich? Learn everything? Spend centuries on a luxury spaceship exploring the Universe? Or maybe relive the past...

## Tomorrow's Times

2 December 3002

### *Lifestyle News*

*Mock-Tudor Takeover*

The Tudor period looks set to become the most popular mock-life craze so far. Seven new villages have been robo-constructed in the last week, and are already fully booked for the next century. Living a lifetime as a Tudor might not sound fun at first, but this is living in history with the nasty bits – smelly toilets, fleas, rotten teeth – all safely removed. Instead, you can enjoy:

Tudor fashion

Tudor cuisine

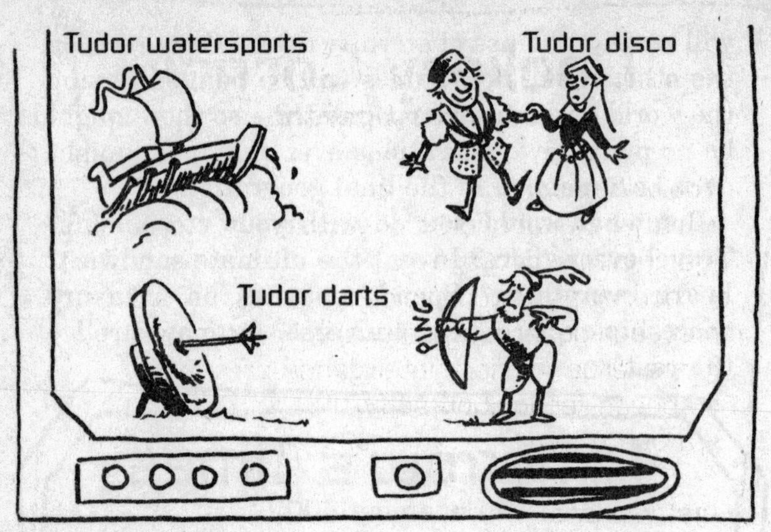


**Live on line**

Guess what? You're already going to live for ever anyway! Right now, loads of information about you is stored on line:

- your medical records;
- results of tests and exams you've taken;
- details of what you buy and where you buy it;
- videos of you (from security cameras);
- recordings of your voice (from voicemail systems);
- emails by, to and about you.

This bank of information about you will grow and grow. Within about 15 years there will be intelligent software that can suss out your personality from your emails, recreate a 3D "you" from recordings of the way you look and sound, and finally give the virtual you a spark of artificial life. This is how it will do it:

# Cookery Corner

## A virtual person

***You will need:***

- lots of digital photos of yourself
- animation software
- recordings of your voice
- speech-generating software
- one large Artificial Intelligence program
- speech-recognition software
- a cup of tea

***Instructions***

**1.** Use the animation software to make a moving 3D outline of a person.

**2.** Feed the photos carefully into the software, positioning them on the outline. Don't worry if you don't have a photo of every bit of your body – just press "calculate" and the software will fill in the gaps, until the 3D outline looks like you.

**3.** Feed the voice recording into the speech-generating software.

**4.** Link the speech-generating software with the animation, so you have a talking version.

**5.** Install the "brain" of the virtual you, by switching on the AI software.

**6.** Switch to "learn" mode. The virtual you will build itself a personality and a memory just like yours – it will find out what it can by checking your old emails and other on-line records, and then use its artificial voice to ask you the questions it needs to fill in any gaps.

**7.** To check the virtual you, try asking your best friend to chat to it. Once they can't tell the difference, your virtual you is ready!

**8.** Relax and drink the tea.

*Next week: how to make a virtual aardvark*

## Everlasting gran

Once your virtual version has been built, there you will be on the Internet and your friends will be able to see and talk to "you" – and "you" will be able to talk back. In the USA, some gravestones already have built-in video screens, which play short clips from the lives of the dead – so "Internet resurrection" is almost bound to catch on as soon as we get the hang of it. So, even if you don't live for ever in the real world and are dead and buried, your descendants will still be able to see you and chat with you, just as if you are still alive. One day, you'll be a resurrected great-great-great-great-grandparent!

And Internet resurrection isn't just for people...

## An icy future

There is a way of living for ever which has already been tested – the only slight snag is, no one is sure yet whether it works on people! Since 1967, a few people have been arranging for themselves to be frozen soon after they die in the hope that in the future it will be possible to defrost them and cure whatever disease it was that polished them off.

Defrosting frozen living things might sound a little bit unlikely, but actually it's not too tricky, at least with small animals. The problem with extending the technique to people is getting the freezing process just right. Human bodies are over 70 per cent water (which makes you wonder why we don't make slopping noises when we run). This means that, if you just stuck a dead person in a freezer, the water would form ice crystals which would swell and crush delicate tissues – especially in the brain. (This is what happens if you freeze and then thaw a watery vegetable like a tomato or a cucumber – try it and see.)

Luckily, ice crystals need time to grow – so, if you can get something cold enough quickly enough, only tiny ones form, and tissues aren't damaged. With a small animal this is easy – it just needs to be dunked in an extremely cold liquid (like helium, which is nearly 300 degrees colder than room temperature).

But this is no good for big things like you and me. If you dunk *us* in liquid helium, the inner parts of our bodies will take quite a while to cool, because they are separated from the helium by such a lot of flesh (not that I'm saying you're fat or anything). However, it will probably be only a matter of time before scientists *do* find a way to freeze people so there is no tissue damage. One method might be to add chemicals to the blood, which will make it solidify into a glassy material rather than ice crystals.

## Oven-ready people

Of course, freezing people without damaging them is only half the problem. How do you defrost them? By warming them very slowly, perhaps by using something like a huge microwave oven (microwaves heat things all the way through rather than just from the outside like conventional ovens). Another method might be to use high-frequency sound waves, which can penetrate and gently warm frozen tissue. The brain would be defrosted first and supplied with blood artificially while the rest of the body was being warmed. When the body was all nice and runny inside, a complete blood transfusion would probably be the easiest way of warming it further and supplying the organs with the nourishment they would need (and would also get rid of the anti-ice-crystal chemicals).

One handy thing about popping yourself in the freezer is that it avoids you eating, breathing or getting very, very bored on long journeys. Actually, this is one of the reasons for researching human freezing in the first place. The journeys the researchers have in mind are very long indeed – all the way to the stars.

# TOMORROW – THE UNIVERSE

For over a century, people who have predicted, imagined or dreamed about the future have predicted, imagined or dreamed about the conquest of space. And quite right too. We might not be quite ready to nip off to Sedna for an ice cream, play space golf in the asteroid belt or soak up the rays on Mercury, but space is definitely the place where the future lies. As a Russian rocket scientist called Konstantin Tsiolkovsky said in 1903:

## Five steps to space

Predicting what our space-shaped future will be like is fairly easy – what is tricky is saying when it will all happen. Whenever it is, scientists reckon there will be five main phases:

**1.** Robotic exploration of the solar system (started in 1959)

**2.** Human exploration of the solar system (started in 1969)

**3.** Permanent human colonies on the Moon, followed by other planets in the solar system (might start in about 2020)

**4.** Robotic exploration of other stars (might start in about 2070)

**5.** Human exploration and colonization of other star systems (might start in about 3000)

***Flashback***

*In 1957, the British Astronomer Royal said, "Space travel is utter bilge." The first space flight took place a few months later.*

## Astrobots

To begin with, the exploration of the Universe won't be carried out by human space-travellers, but by intelligent robots. This will certainly be a lot cheaper, since the ships will be able to accelerate faster, won't need air or warmth or cooling, will be able to travel for decades with no complaints from the crew and will never need to return to Earth.

Actually, robots have already had a stab at exploring space themselves – and been much more successful than people.

Well, *generally* more successful...

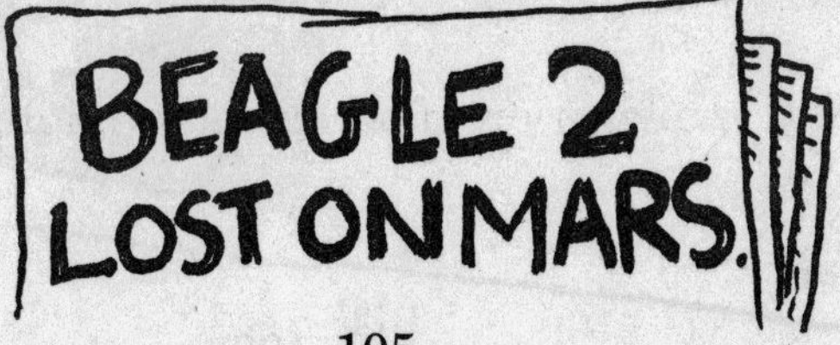

Space robotics is a huge subject, but here are some of the types of robot built to boldly go where nobot has gone before:

**Type:** Space probe

**Missions:** Fly-bys and crash-landings on planets and other solar-system objects, explorations of deep space

**Typical functions:** Sending images back to Earth, measuring radiation levels

**Have explored:**

- all the planets in the solar system except Pluto
- all the large moons in the solar system except Charon (Pluto's moon)
- several asteroids and comets

**First successful version:**

**Country:** USSR

**Name:** Luna I

**Destination:** the Moon

**Launch date:** 2 January 1959

**Type:** Orbiter

**Missions:** Orbiting Sun, planets or moons

**Typical functions:** Measuring radiation levels, photographic mapping, radar mapping, communicating with rovers

**Have explored:**

- Sun
- Moon
- Venus
- Mars
- Saturn

**First successful version:**

**Country:** USA

**Name:** Pioneer 6

**Studied:** the Sun

**Launch Date:** 16 December 1965

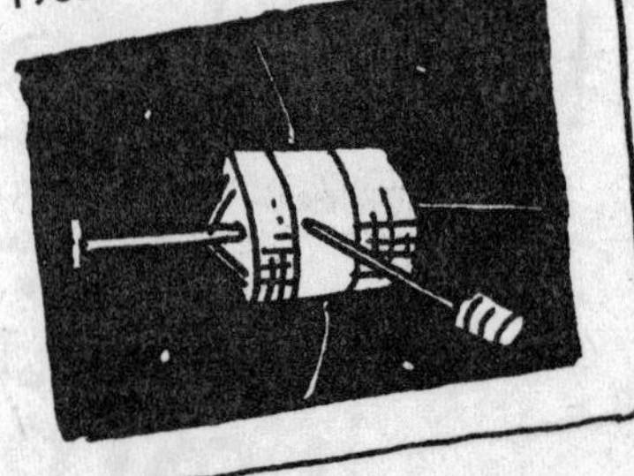

**Type:** Lander

**Missions:** Soft-landings on planets or moons

**Typical functions:** Sending images back to Earth, chemical tests of soil, measurement of earthquakes and magnetic fields

**Have explored:**

- Moon
- Mars
- Venus

**First successful version:**

**Country:** USSR

**Name:** Luna 9

**Destination:** the Moon

**Launch Date:** 31 January 1966

**Type:** Rover

**Missions:** Exploration of surfaces of planets or moons

**Typical functions:** Sending images back to Earth, investigating rocks, soil and surface features

**Have explored:**

- Moon
- Mars

**First successful version:**

**Country:** USSR

**Name:** Lunokhod 1

**Destination:** the Moon

**Launch Date:** 10 November 1970

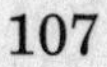

## The human factor

So, robots are jolly good at exploring space, what with being ever so tough, not having to breathe, and not minding the fact that they don't get to go back to Earth again.

But, then again, there's nothing we humans like more than a spot of exploration (some of us anyway) – there was no good reason to climb Everest or land on the Moon, yet both these things are dead popular, despite the risk of coming to a sticky end. So it seems almost certain we will eventually explore the Universe in person.

If you fancy doing this yourself, what you could do with is a type of engine that could get you to the nearest star in a few minutes – as almost all space-travel films show happening. But put down that Argos catalogue – as far as we know, this is impossible, because nothing in the Universe can travel faster than light – and light takes over four years to reach the nearest star.

## Slow lane to space

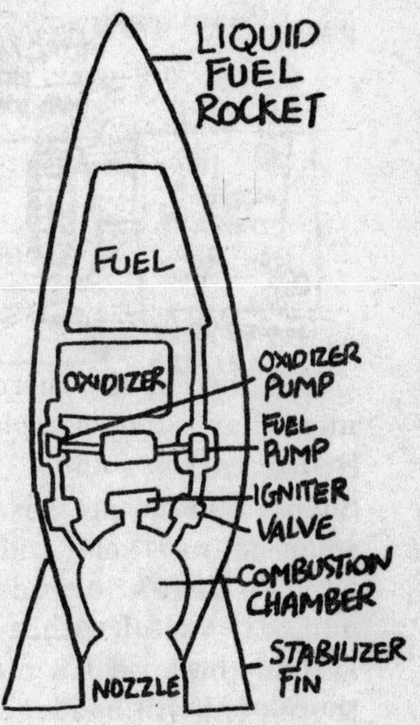


But that doesn't mean we won't ever explore the Universe ourselves – in fact, spaceships to take us anywhere in the solar system could be built right now, using basically the same technology that got people to the Moon in 1969: liquid-fuel rockets.

This method would be *terribly* slow and expensive though, so it's just as well that several new spaceship drive systems have been designed and tested already, and there are more which haven't quite made it off the drawing-board yet. These are the main ones...

### Solar-powered ion drive

This works by breaking up molecules (of anything you like – water would be handy), and generating thrust* by shooting the bits (called ions) into space by using an electric field. An electric field is like a

* Thrust is how hard a drive can push a spaceship through space.

magnetic field (as used to support maglevs – see page 77), but instead of pulling or pushing magnets, an electric field pulls or pushes things which are electrically charged – like the bits of broken-up molecules. The power is supplied by solar cells (see page 67).

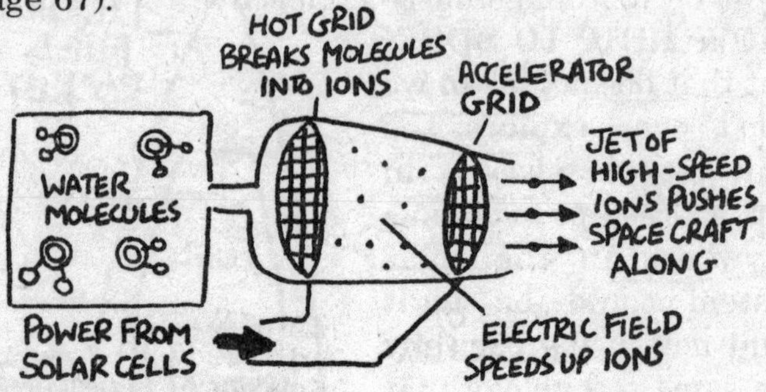


## Solar sail

Solar radiation presses on everything it touches. A solar sail uses solar radiation like a yacht uses the wind, so there's no need to carry fuel. It is quite slow and only useful within the inner part of the solar system (because it's nice and sunny all the time there), but will be ideal for carrying heavy loads to space colonies.

## Nuclear thermal drive

In this drive system, a nuclear reactor (see page 65) is used to convert water to super-heated steam to provide thrust. It can produce a lot more power than the chemical rockets that we use today, but might be too dangerously radioactive to use near the Earth.

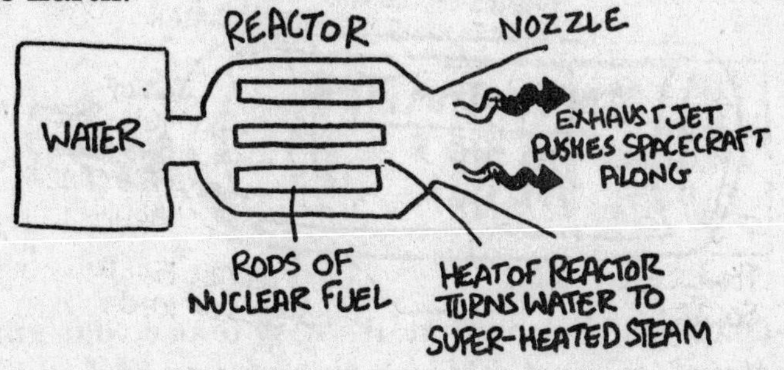


## Matter/anti-matter engines

These are what they use on Star Trek! I must admit that we don't know quite how to make them yet, but they should be *great* once we get the hang of them. Anti-matter is a sort of mirror image of ordinary matter – it looks the same, but if it comes into contact with ordinary matter (you, for example), it, and the ordinary matter, vanish in an enormous burst of energy, far more powerful than even a nuclear blast. It's tricky stuff to make and even trickier to store – you can't keep it in a bottle made of ordinary matter, for obvious reasons. But scientists do have some idea of how to do both.

To make anti-matter, you can just smack ordinary matter really really hard into more ordinary matter. The matter atoms are smashed to pieces, and some of these pieces are pieces of anti-matter.

To keep anti-matter, what you need is a bottle – with an inside that generates an electric field. So the inside pushes away the electrically-charged anti-matter without touching it. Once you've made your anti-matter, you can use an electric field to move it around, and to pop it into its bottle. Not forgetting to put the lid on.

Once you've done that, it's easy to use your anti-matter fuel – just release a tiny amount of it and as soon as it touches normal matter there'll be a huge burst of energy – just the ticket for shoving your spaceship off into outer space.

## Interstellar ramjet

The space between the stars isn't empty. It contains a very thin scattering of broken-up atoms of a gas called hydrogen. This is an ideal fuel for a fusion reactor (page 68), and it could be collected by using yet another electric field. In an interstellar ramjet, a field many thousands of kilometres wide sweeps up the electrically charged bits of hydrogen and funnels them to the reactor, which uses the hydrogen as fuel and pushes the spaceship along (and also supplies the energy to generate the field). A small amount of fuel (or some other type of drive) would probably be included, to get the ramjet up to a high enough speed so that it could sweep up enough hydrogen to get going.

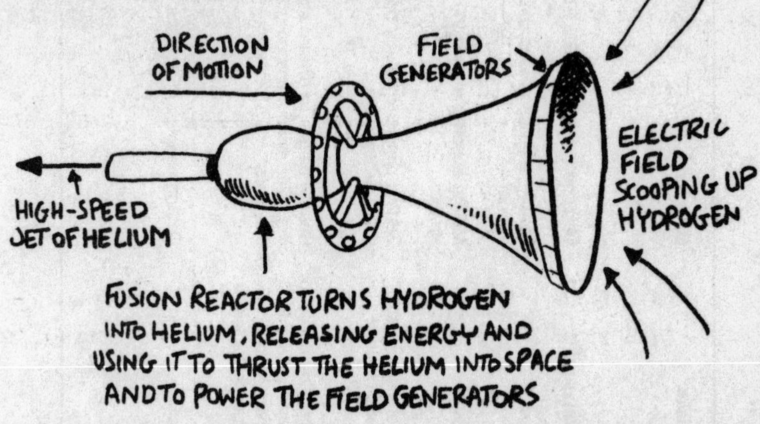


So, which sort of drive system will future astronauts really use? Probably all of them – they all have their pros and cons. Unlike planes, it doesn't mean much to say how fast a spaceship can go. In space, once a vessel is well away from the Sun and planets, there is no gravity or anything else to slow it down, so enormous speeds can be reached – eventually. What counts is how *long* it takes to reach a reasonable speed, which depends on the thrust of the drive. Plenty of thrust is also needed to take off from a planet.

Another important factor is how much fuel a spaceship needs to carry. The big problem with liquid fuel is that it's heavy (it made up more than 90 per cent of the weight of the spaceship that took people to the Moon).

So, if you want to be an astronaut in the future, the drive you'll choose will depend on what you want to do and where you want to go:

| | Thrust | Amount of on-board fuel needed | Cost | Risks | Best for |
|---|---|---|---|---|---|
| **Liquid-fuel rocket** | High | Huge | High | Can explode | Getting off planets |
| **Solar-powered ion drive** | Medium | Not much | Medium | Low | Moving supplies around the solar system |
| **Solar sail** | Low | None at all | Low | Low | Moving supplies around the solar system |
| **Nuclear thermal drive** | High | Quite a lot | High | Radioactive (so can't be used near Earth) | Getting people to nearby parts of the solar system |
| **Matter/anti-matter drive** | Very high | Not much | Very high | Slight tendency to destroy itself in phenomenally gigantic explosion | Getting people to distant parts of the solar system and cargoes to the stars |
| **Interstellar ramjet** | Increases the faster it goes | Hardly any | Very high | Low | Getting people to the stars |

With one of these nifty drives up your sleeve (or more likely in your spaceship), you'll be free to conquer the galaxy – or just go there on your hols.

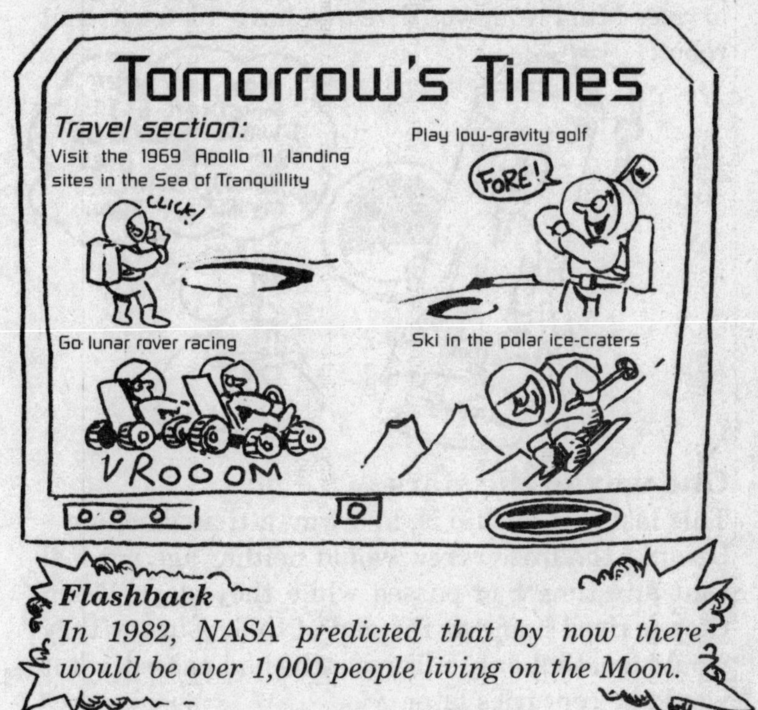


***Flashback***

*In 1982, NASA predicted that by now there would be over 1,000 people living on the Moon.*

## Are we nearly there yet?

Even the fastest spacecraft we can imagine will take many years to travel even to nearby stars. How would people cope? One possibility for very long journeys is a generation starship – a flying city in which generations of people could live and die on the journey. It's a bit hard to imagine people flocking excitedly to sign up for that sort of mission though, so a more likely idea is the sort of freezing process we looked at in the last chapter (page 101):

the crew would be frozen before they leave, and robots would keep an eye on them during the journey, and then help to thaw them out when they arrive. Mind you, you'd *really* have to trust that robot!

## One way to the stars

This last sort of ship is, in a way, a time machine – because the frozen crew would neither age nor feel that any time had passed while they slept. When they arrived home at the end of their journey they would feel that only a few months had passed, yet it would be centuries later.

That's one reason why, once people arrive on an Earth-like distant planet, they won't come home again. Instead, they'll build a colony. However, it's very *very* unlikely that they will be able to breathe the air, so the colonists will need to make their own breathable air, and seal themselves off from the planet's atmosphere – perhaps by building, or inflating, a transparent dome.

Making breathable air to keep in the dome will be easy. The air you breathe in is partly made of a gas called oxygen. In your lungs, some of the oxygen is removed from the air (and comes in very handy for all sorts of things that go on inside you). This oxygen is replaced with a waste gas called carbon dioxide, which you then breathe out. The reason why the Earth's oxygen doesn't get used up by us breathing it in all the time is that plants do just the opposite – they take in carbon dioxide and give out oxygen.

Space colonies are likely to use both chemical systems and plants to make breathable air (not to mention lunch). So, for your space-travelling descendants, home might look like this...

The first such colony will almost certainly be on the Moon, and the second on Mars. But, at least on Mars, the colonists and their descendants may not have to live under their domes for ever. They might remake their bodies (using the techniques in the last chapter) and turn themselves into Martians who can survive out on the surface.

## Unearthly world

Compared to the Earth, Mars is icy cold, scorched with deadly radiation, and has a low gravity. The air is very thin indeed, with practically no oxygen. So it's not exactly what you'd call a homely planet.

| | Earth | Mars |
|---|---|---|
| Length of day | 24 hours | 24.5 hours |
| Length of year | 365 days | 687 days |
| Average temperature | 15°C | -50°C |
| Air pressure | 1 atmosphere | 0.006 atmosphere |
| Oxygen in the air | 21% | 0.1% |
| Weight of this book | 140 g | 54 g |

## Life on Mars

To venture on to the surface of Mars without a spacesuit, you would need a new type of skin – resistant to radiation and tough enough to stop your body swelling in the low pressure (the higher pressure inside our bodies is similar to that on Earth, because that's where they evolved). A machine of some sort would probably be needed to store oxygen, and might feed it directly into your bloodstream, so you wouldn't actually breathe at all. Your eyes would need to be coated with plastic to keep out the radiation, and built-in radio would replace speech (which you can't make if you don't breathe and which would sound very faint in the thin air anyway).

Making all these changes would turn you into a cross between a robot and a walking spacesuit – in fact, you might look just like the sort of Martian that used to menace the earthlings in 1950s science-fiction films. Just in case you aren't particularly thrilled with the prospect, don't worry – it's possible that, instead of making ourselves suitable for life on Mars, we'll make Mars suitable for us: by terraforming it.

# Makeovers in space

Terraforming means remaking a planet. Sounds tricky? Well, yes, it is actually. But it might well be possible, and Mars could be an ideal candidate. The main reason it's so inhospitable is that it has such a thin atmosphere. Atmospheres are like duvets – they keep warmth in. Giving Mars the right atmosphere should be enough to make it, if not quite like Earth, at least similar enough to make living there easier.

So the next question is – where can you get a nice thick warm atmosphere for a planet? Luckily, Mars has one tucked away already – in the form of frozen carbon dioxide gas at its poles.

So, all we need to do is warm Mars gently and we'll be well on the way to an atmosphere. We could do it like this...

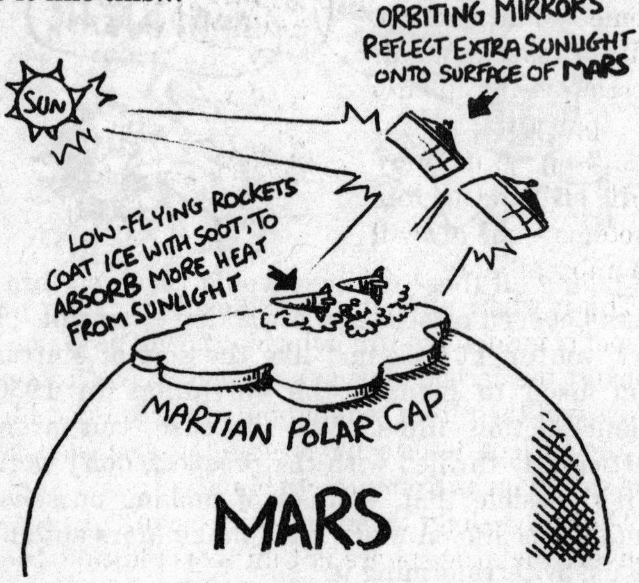

Once the air starts to thicken, we'll need to add some more "greenhouse gases" to warm it up. These are chemicals which trap heat – carbon dioxide is a greenhouse gas itself, but there are even better ones that could be made from the Martian soil.

## New blue planet

Making Mars warm won't just make it airier and comfier – it will also make it wetter. Water is vital for life, and water vapour is yet another greenhouse gas. Luckily, Mars has shedloads of the stuff, in the form of ice under the soil. As the atmosphere warms, this ice will melt and the atmosphere will get damper and warmer still – eventually, rivers and lakes may appear, and Mars will turn a bit blue.

By this time, Mars will be a lot more like home – fairly warm, with a reasonable air pressure and plenty of opportunities for paddling. But there will still be a big problem – the air will be unbreathable.

This is where all that carbon dioxide, together with a spot of gardening, will help: plants will be grown to convert the carbon dioxide to oxygen. In the process, Mars will turn from red-and-blue to green-and-blue, as the ancient deserts are covered by vegetation, and the sky changes from pink to blue.

The only slight problem with using plants to convert the atmosphere is that it would take them about 500 years. But by the time people are ready to turn Mars into an Earth-like planet, nanobots (page 72) will probably be on the case, too. They will float on the Martian breezes, absorbing carbon dioxide and releasing oxygen.

After a bit more messing about (like releasing a gas called nitrogen from the soil), the solar system's biggest chemistry experiment will be finished and the Martian people will be able to do all the things you *can* do on a nice new planet, such as farming, city-building and...

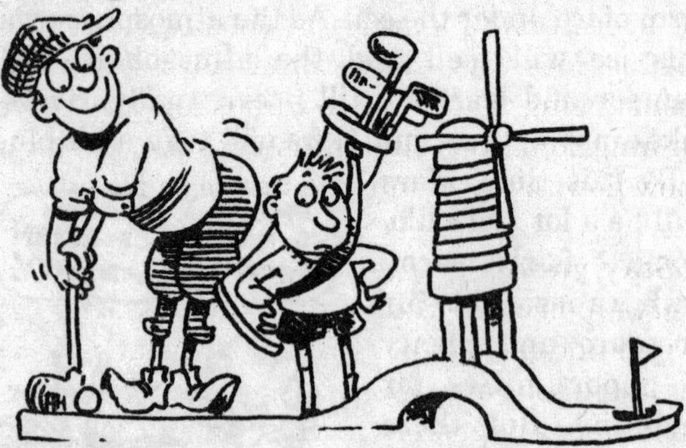

Since the Universe is really rather large, with plenty of planets just waiting to be landed on, exploration, colonization, terraforming and body modification will almost certainly occupy most of our future. Among other things, this will mean that, instead of only surviving as long as the Earth does, the human race will probably last as long as the stars.

Quite apart from all the stars and planets there are to explore (about as many as there are grains of sand on all the beaches in all the countries of the

Earth – plenty, in other words), there is also a whole new area of exploration for us. Not the universe of stars, but the universe of time...

## Travelling to tomorrow

In 1905 Albert Einstein discovered a way to travel into the future – in fact, being a genius, he discovered two ways in which we're actually doing it already! As we'll see in a minute, both motion and weight change the rate at which time passes, so you can use either effect to make a time machine. Even the speed and weights we're used to affect the flow of time. Not very much, mind you, so don't worry about being eaten by a dinosaur while you're running for a bus. But Einstein's work means we know how to travel into the future as far as we like:

**1. Stay young: go fast**

Einstein discovered time-travel not by carrying out some mind-blowingly expensive experiment, nor by doing millions of calculations, but by imagining just what would happen to a collection of clocks as they rushed about all over the place. To understand his discovery, all you need to do is imagine a very simple clock yourself, like this:

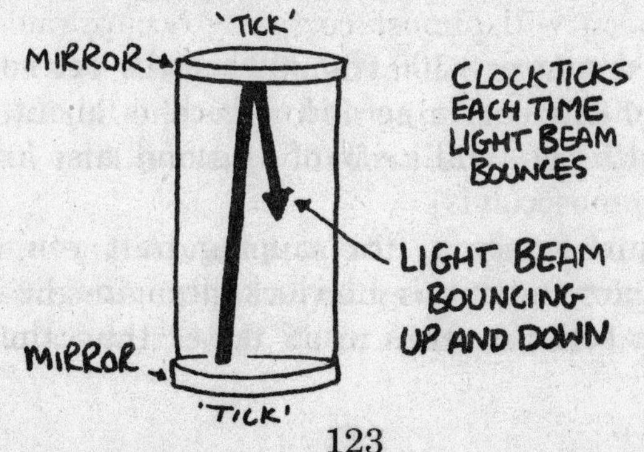

The clock is simply a light beam shuttling up and down between a pair of mirrors. The clock ticks each time the beam bounces.

We, and Einstein, also need a simple rule, a law of nature which has been proved many times by all sorts of experiments. The rule is:

**LIGHT ALWAYS TRAVELS AT 300 MILLION METRES A SECOND, NO MATTER WHO MEASURES IT**

Imagine your best mate Eric has got a light clock. He can work out how often the clock ticks, if he knows how long it is. If it's a metre long, the time for the light beam to move from one mirror to another is given by a very simple equation:

TIME = DISTANCE ÷ SPEED

Which means in this case:

TIME = 1 metre ÷ 300,000,000 metres per second = 1/300,000,000 of a second (which is about 3.33 thousandths of a millionth of a second, also known as 3.33 nanoseconds).

Now, just imagine Eric zipping past you on a rocket, carrying his light clock. Imagine he goes past you several times, each faster than the one before. You'll see the light beam tracing a zigzag pattern like this:

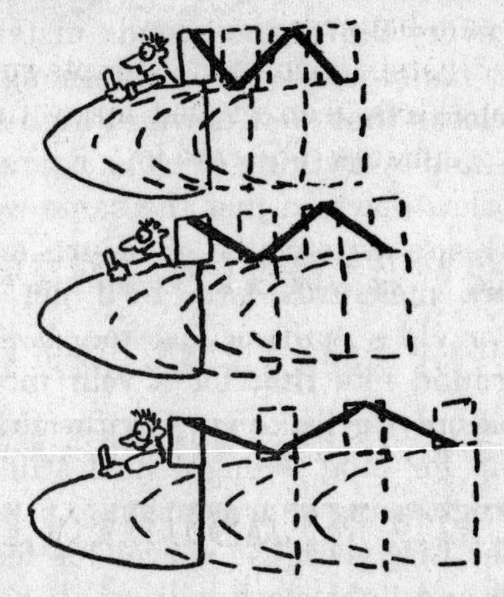

The faster Eric goes, the flatter the zigzag will get. Look at the length of each zig or zag. You'll see that each is longer than the length of the clock. In the last cartoon, each zig is twice as long as the clock.

Now, let's go back to our equation again:

TIME = DISTANCE ÷ SPEED

We can find out how fast the clock in the last cartoon is ticking, now that the light is moving twice as far between ticks (and bearing in mind that, thanks to the rule on page 124, the light's speed is the same as before).

TIME = 2 metres ÷ 300,000,000 metres per second = 2/300,000,000 of a second (which is about 6.67 nanoseconds).

So, now we know that the clock in the last cartoon ticks half as fast as it does when it's standing still – only once every 6.67 nanoseconds instead of once every 3.33 nanoseconds. Weirdly enough, it's not just light clocks that slow down at high speeds, it's all clocks – and everything else too. Eric's heart and mind will slow down in just the same way. So, not only will Eric's wristwatch measure one minute while yours measures two, he'll get sleepy or hungry – or old – half as fast too. If he goes on rushing around like that for a year (according to you), it will only feel like six months to him. If he keeps going for long enough, he'll still be young when you're drawing your pension.

The faster Eric goes, the slower his feelings and wristwatch and light clock will get. If he goes fast enough, a year as measured by you will feel like one day to him. Faster still, and a year for you will be a second for him. He does have to go very fast indeed to do this, mind you – not far off the speed of light itself, in fact.

This all means that high-speed Eric is now a time-traveller. To find out how the world is in a century, he just has to wait 100 seconds. In an hour (according to his wristwatch), he'll be over 3,000 years in the future, and in one of his days he'll travel through 86,000 years!

The problem with this sort of time-travel is that it takes a ginormous amount of fuel to speed someone up to such a high speed. Luckily, Einstein (who really was terribly clever) found another way to time-travel a few years later...

### 2. Stay young: get heavy

Einstein's second way to time-travel is easier in one way and trickier in two others. He found that the pull of gravity slowed down time.* So that means, all you have to do is go to a place with a very strong gravity pull, and lurk about there for a while. No rushing around required. The tricky things are **a)** getting to a high-gravity place and **b)** dragging yourself away again. But the sort of advanced spaceships we were talking about earlier in the chapter could do the trick. And scientists have already found plenty of high-gravity places to go.

With all that time-travel nicely discovered, no wonder Einstein once said:

* Sadly, there's no space to explain quite why here, but you could always have a look at *Dead Famous: Albert Einstein and his Inflatable Universe* to find out all about it.

### 3. Bringing back yesterday

Both of Einstein's time machines have one big problem – they can only make one-way trips through time. So, given enough speed, or gravity, you can explore the year AD 3000 without hanging about for nearly a thousand years first, but once you're there, you can't get back. And Einstein's time machines don't allow you to reach the year 3000 BC – or AD 2000 for that matter, either. So, though you can travel through time to check whether I got my facts right when I wrote this book, you won't be able to return to the 21st century to tell me I didn't. Sadly.

There *is* a possible type of time machine which offers return tickets to the future, but it couldn't take you back to a time before it was built – and building it will take technology we're not likely to develop for many centuries. It involves a combination of high gravity and rapid spin, and it might look a bit like this:

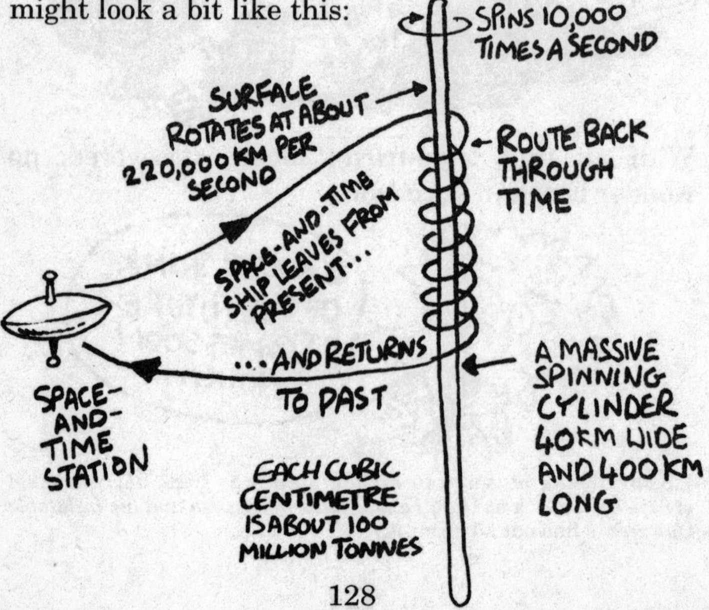

## Ways of escape

Why, you may be asking yourself, would the people of the future want to colonize Mars, travel in time or explore outer space anyway? After all, what with all the wonderful homes, amazing cities, gorgeous gizmos and fantastic virtual worlds they'll have, what more could they want? Well, it has to be said that the future won't *all* be fun. It has a few nasty surprises up its sleeves, including a whole range of ways in which big chunks of the world's population might be wiped out. After you've read the next chapter, you might think that nipping off to another planet, even one with frozen air, a lot of volcanoes, or an alien monster or two, is a lot more attractive than the sort of thing that might happen to you if you stay at home...

# NIGHTMARE TOMORROWS

If you're of a nervous disposition – the sort of person who worries about monsters under the bed or invasions from space – it might be best to give this chapter a miss. As we saw on page 89, the Earth will probably lose all its oceans by the year two billion and have its surface destroyed by the year five billion. But, unless they colonize other planets first, human beings might not last anything like that long. The future is a dangerous place, full of terrifying dangers that might mean the end of civilization, or of human beings, or even of all life on Earth.

You might be interested to hear that it's happened before – 65 million years ago the dinosaurs, which dominated the Earth as successfully then as we do now and for far, far longer, were almost completely wiped out, almost certainly by an asteroid strike. And, in 250000000 BC, 96 per cent of all the species that then existed were destroyed by a mysterious worldwide disaster that no one has been able to explain. These things happen. They'll happen again.

## The long summer

With the Millennium Bug out of the way, the biggest issue in futurology at the moment is global warming. All scientists agree that it is happening, and almost all agree it is due to an increase in pollution in the atmosphere, which traps the Sun's heat.

If temperatures rise high enough to melt the polar ice-caps, sea levels will rise by at least 80 metres – putting London, Paris and many other cities underwater.

But there is a big debate about when global warming will start to cause serious problems: some scientists predict that it will cause widespread flooding of low-lying areas within decades, others think it will take much longer. The good news is that global warming can still be stopped, simply by cutting the production of the pollutants that cause it. The bad news is that many countries show no sign of cutting pollutants enough to make much of a difference.

But compared with some of the other things that are likely to happen to us, global warming is not a major problem. The rest of this chapter looks at some ways the world could end...

**Event:** asteroid impact

**The facts:** the solar system is full of drifting chunks of rock, some bigger than skyscrapers. From time to time, these objects pass near the Earth, and are dragged down by the planet's gravity.

The resulting crashes can cause huge dust-storms that last for months, cutting off the warmth of the Sun, as well as instant local devastation. The next known possible collision is on 7 August 2046, when asteroid 1999AN10 has a 1-in-500,000 chance of crashing into the Earth.

**Probability of this happening in next 100 years:** 1 in 10,0000

**World's population killed:** 25%

**The fix:** we can do a lot – depending on how long we have between discovering the asteroid and it hitting us, and on how big it is. Nuclear bombs seem the most likely way of deflecting asteroids at the moment, delivered by long-range rockets. Other possible solutions include blowing asteroids up, or spinning them so fast they tear themselves apart.

**Event:** plague

**The facts:** a deadly epidemic, as easy to catch as a cold, but fatal. It could either be natural, or something deliberately developed by terrorists or part of a world war.

**Probability of this happening in next 100 years:** 1 in 100

**World's population killed:** up to 70%

**The fix:** scientists will isolate themselves and have a good chance of finding a cure – though this will take too long to save many people. Also, some people are likely to develop a natural immunity. Border controls may save whole countries, but only if the guards are prepared to slaughter all the thousands who try to enter.

**Event:** nuclear war

**The facts:** several countries have nuclear weapons – enough to kill everyone in the world several times over. So far, only two relatively small and primitive atomic bombs have been used in war (in 1945, against Japan).

**Probability of this happening in next 100 years:** 1 in 50

**World's population killed:** 80%

**The fix:** a few decades ago, it was thought that a nuclear war was quite likely – a 1 in 3 chance, maybe. But many countries have now reduced their supplies of nuclear weapons, so war is less likely. On the other hand, many more countries have weapons now, so there is still a chance of nuclear war.

**Event:** giant volcano

**The facts:** in the distant past, whole continents seem to have been devastated by super-volcanoes called calderas, but it's not known what triggers the eruptions. The most recent massive eruption happened in AD 535 – as a result, the world's climate cooled for years, and there was plague, famine and mass migrations of people. The collapse of the Roman Empire was probably at least partly due to this volcano. A caldera eruption would destroy the country it happened in, and the vast clouds of dust and smoke that followed could cut off sunlight and freeze the rest of the planet.

**Probability of this happening in next 100 years:** 1 in 500
**World's population killed:** 10%
**The fix:** only to evacuate affected areas, though this will save only a small fraction of the victims. There may be warnings days or even months before the eruption, if there are disturbances in the Earth's interior which seismologists (scientists who measure earth tremors) can detect.

**Event:** collapse of ozone layer

**The facts:** the ozone layer already has a gaping hole in it over the southerly parts of the Earth's southern hemisphere. The hole lets deadly radiation through from the Sun, and as a result skin cancer deaths have grown, but the whole layer isn't going to collapse as was once feared (see below).

**Probability of this happening in next 100 years:** 0%

**World's population killed:** up to 1% if the hole is allowed to grow, but...

**The fix:** we're fixing it already (thanks to futurology)! The ozone hole is formed by pollutants that used to be used in aerosols and refrigerators – these have now been banned and, slowly, the hole should close again as more ozone is produced naturally. By 2100, it should be completely gone.

**Event:** Robot rebellion



**The facts:** some scientists think that, as the intelligence of robots increases further, a time will come (maybe as soon as 2050) when they become cleverer than us and decide to take over.
**Probability of this happening in next 100 years:** unknown
**Fraction of world's population killed:** unknown
**The fix:** As robotic intelligence increases and they become less dependent on us (and we become more dependent on them), only well-enforced laws about their development can help.

Of course, that isn't a complete list of the ways the world might end – there could be a nanobot-virus that converts everything to sludge, the Sun might flare up and roast us or fade and freeze us. We might even be invaded from outer space!

In case this all makes you think that next week might contain even worse things than school, have a look back at the probabilities – it's very unlikely any worldwide disaster will happen in your lifetime.

The effects of a major catastrophe on the human race as a whole will depend on when it happens. It may not be until we have colonies on the Moon and Mars, miners in the asteroid belt, and frozen astronauts on deep-space missions who could rebuild and repopulate the Earth, even if all life here is annihilated.

The rescuers might face some competition when they land, though – the Earth might well have been overrun by rats or cockroaches or robots or spiders, all of which can cope better with disasters than we can. They might have become a lot more clever, numerous and dangerous by then, too.

Or maybe people won't *want* to rebuild the Earth and will be happy to leave it to the rats and robots. We can't assume that people in the future will think like us any more than we can assume they'll look like us: attitudes and beliefs have changed enormously even over the last few decades. Imagine how much more they might change over the next few million years!

There are lots of things to look forward to in your own future, from the arrival of the first humans on Mars, to chatty computers and films that happen all around you – so, though it might be fearful and frightening at times, your future really *is* going to be fun, flabbergasting, fabulous and fantastic. And it starts now.

# FACE THE FUTURE

Try this fiendishly futuristic quiz – and look into your own future by predicting how many answers (out of 17) you'll get right before you look at the questions...

**1.** The Sun will have gone out in
**a)** a hundred million years
**b)** a thousand million years
**c)** a million million years

**2.** Space probes from Earth
**a)** have already visited Neptune
**b)** will visit Neptune in about AD 2500
**c)** will visit Neptune in about AD 4000

**3.** There will be a total eclipse of the Sun in
**a)** 2018
**b)** 2019
**c)** 2020

**4.** Terraforming is
**a)** changing a planet to make it more habitable
**b)** making scary virtual-reality adventures
**c)** building new types of living creature

**5.** Cyborg stands for
**a)** CYbernetic ORGanism
**b)** CitY Building by Organized Robotic Groups
**c)** Cell Youth By Retro-active Genetics

**6.** Which type of spaceship could get to the stars quickest?
**a)** solar-powered ion drive
**b)** anti-matter drive
**c)** solar sail

**7.** In a century, the Earth's population is likely to be
**a)** about half today's
**b)** about the same as today's
**c)** about twice today's

**8.** Computer power tends to double every
**a)** 18 weeks
**b)** 18 months
**c)** 18 years

**9.** Weather forecasts are often wrong because
**a)** the weather is a chaotic system
**b)** computers aren't powerful enough yet
**c)** there aren't enough weather satellites yet

**10.** The butterfly effect is all about
**a)** butterflies
**b)** chaos
**c)** flight

**11.** In about 5,000,000,000 years
**a)** the Sun will turn red and swell up
**b)** the Sun will turn black and explode
**c)** the Sun will turn green and collapse

**12.** The Millennium Bug was
**a)** an illness
**b)** an insect
**c)** a computer problem

**13.** What is MEMS short for?
**a)** Magneto-Electric Monitoring Systems
**b)** MicroElectroMechanical Systems
**c)** MElody Modifying Software

**14.** Where gravity is strong (like near a black hole), time passes
**a)** faster than on the Earth
**b)** more slowly than on the Earth
**c)** the same speed as on the Earth

**15.** MAGLEV is short for
**a)** Micro-Atomic Gravitationally-assisted Long-rangE Vehicle
**b)** MAGnetic LEVitation
**c)** Mentally And Genetically controlLEd Volunteer

**16.** About five new babies are born
**a)** every second
**b)** every minute
**c)** every hour

**17.** What type of stars can be white, red, brown or black?
**a)** black holes
**b)** dwarf stars
**c)** giant stars

**Answers:**
**1c)** (page 89)
**2a)** (page 106)
**3c)** (page 14)
**4a)** (page 120)
**5a)** (page 96)
**6b)** (page 111)
**7c)** (page 17)
**8b)** (page 17)
**9a)** (page 22)
**10b)** (page 21)
**11a)** (page 89)
**12c)** (page 19)
**13b)** (page 10)
**14b)** (page 127)
**15b)** (page 77)
**16a)** (page 17)
**17b)** (pages 89 and 90)

# THE FUTURE'S OUT THERE...

...in these films, books and websites:

**Films**

*Metropolis*, 1926: a chilling vision of a futuristic city stalked by a deadly robot.

*Things to Come*, 1936: how your grandparents' generation thought the world might look in 1940, the 1960s and 2036.

*Forbidden Planet*, 1956: in the 23rd century, our space-travelling descendants face a yet more futuristic civilization.

*The Time Machine*, 1960: a trip from 1900 to the year AD 802701, stopping off at 1917, 1940 and 1966 on the way.

*Planet of the Apes*, 1968: astronauts of the future explore an alien planet – with a twist.

*2001, A Space Odyssey*, 1968: sadly, space travel wasn't quite that advanced in the real 2001. But the computer-controlled freezer-ship is likely to be built one day.

*Bladerunner*, 1982: a hunt for murderous androids in a run-down future.

*Tron*, 1982: an early vision of a virtual-reality world.

*Minority Report*, 2002: a scary future just round the corner.

*Terminator 3*, 2003: a future war against killer machines.

## Books

*Green Files: Future Power*, Steve Parker, Heinemann Library, 2003
*Eyewitness Guide: Future*, Michael Tambini, Dorling Kindersley, 2002
*The Kingfisher Encyclopedia of the Future*, Anthony Wilson and Clive Gifford, Kingfisher, 2001
*Guinness Amazing Future*, Mark Fletcher, Guinness World Records Ltd, 1999

## Websites

The latest scientific inventions and discoveries are at:
http://www.bbc.co.uk/science/
and
www.popsci.com

NASA's future missions:
http://spacescience.nasa.gov/missions/

Science museum:
www.sciencemuseum.org.uk